HERMANN HESSE

HERMANN HESSE

An Illustrated Biography

Bernhard Zeller

Translated by Mark Hollebone

PETER OWEN · LONDON

ISBN 0 7206 0262 9

Original edition: *Hermann Hesse, in Selbstzeugnissen und Bild-dokumenten.* © 1963 by Rowohlt Taschenbuch Verlag

The publishers are grateful to Jonathan Cape Ltd for permission to reprint excerpts from the English language editions of: *The Glass Bead Game,* translated by Richard and Clara Winston; *Poems* (by Hermann Hesse), selected and translated by James Wright; and *Klingsor's Last Summer,* translated by Richard and Clara Winston.

PETER OWEN LIMITED
12 Kendrick Mews Kendrick Place London SW7

First published by Peter Owen Ltd 1972
English translation © 1971 by Herder & Herder Ltd

Printed in Great Britain by
Lowe & Brydone (Printers) Ltd
Victoria Road London NW10

CONTENTS

The Nobel Prize Winner (1946).

ANCESTRY AND CHILDHOOD

"I cannot tell my story without reaching a long way back. If it were possible I would go back farther still—into the very first years of my childhood, and beyond them into distant ancestral past." Those are the opening words of the Prologue to Hermann Hesse's novel *Demian* (1919), and they apply equally well to whomever would tell its author's own story, for throughout his life and work Hesse kept his origins, childhood, and youth continually in mind. In *Hermann Lauscher,* an early work (1901), Hesse wrote, "Writers, more than other men, have recourse to their earliest memories," and he himself never tired of telling of the awakening of his childhood consciousness, of his experience of youth, and of the inner conflicts he struggled with as he grew towards maturity. Few writers have paid so much attention to the child's consciousness or have given the problems of education and character formation such central roles in their literary output.

Again and again, and even in old age, Hesse dreamed himself back into his sacred childhood world, and in his works frequently conjured up memories of his parents and grandparents, teachers and friends, describing with a passion and sensibility no biographer could ever achieve the details of his childhood landscape with its river, its bridge, and its gable-roofed houses. On his sickbed in Sils Maria, the eighty-year-old's thoughts returned to his birthplace, attempting to recall its appearance house by house. "Leafing through my scrapbook, conjuring up, contemplating, and arranging the treasury of pictures my

7

memory snapped in former times" became a consciously enacted game which disclosed new things, and brought him the joy of recovering what he had thought lost.

But reflecting on the years of youth and childhood was not only a harmless game played with the "sunlit past," but also the most important ingredient of a literary output whose objective was the formulation and penetration through literature of the writer's own world of sense and experience. "My purpose is to delineate that piece of humanity and love, of instinct and sublimation, that I know of from my own experience, and for whose truth, sincerity, and actuality I can vouch." Hesse's writing is self-portrayal and self-analysis, a continuous and watchful debate with himself; it is a poetical and humane self-confession that has few equals in twentieth-century literature. Consciously, Hesse restricted his writings to what he could draw from his own immediate environment and from his own experience of life. He wrote no historical novels, nor even contemporary ones. He sought no material that was not a consequence of first-hand experience, and had no interest in constructing new fragments of reality as is usual in imaginative literature. He was not concerned with the social problems of the modern world, but deeply with the individual's problems in that world. Through self-involvement and the elucidation of personal detail, he expanded the compass of inner reality beyond the merely autobiographical, and by revealing his own intellectual and spiritual constitution, did the same in part for that of our own times.

Hesse has left us neither diary nor memoirs. Nor, beyond two short autobiographical sketches ("Kurzgefassten Lebenslauf"—"Curriculum Vitae"; and "Kindheit des Zauberers"—"The Magician's Childhood"), did he leave us an account of his life. But much of what he wrote tells us clearly about himself. *Kurgast (Patient)* and *Nürn-*

8

Birthplace in Calw.

berger Reise (Journey to Nuremberg) relate his own experiences, and—in an important sense—most of his poetry
and his novels are fragments of a large-scale self-portrait,
contributions to a personal confession. With these at our
disposal, additional sources are hardly necessary. The
details of the writer's inner and public life can be sifted
from his writings. Indeed, they are inseparable.

Hermann Hesse was born in 1877 in Calw, a small town
in the northern region of the Black Forest. His father,
Johannes Hesse, born in 1847, was a doctor's son and
came from Estland. His mother, Marie Gundert, was born
in India, the daughter of a missionary. The Hesse family

9

was of Baltic German descent; the Gunderts were Swabians (though Marie Gundert's father married a girl who was part Welsh and part Swiss). The two families had met through their common involvement in missionary work. Hermann Gundert, the father, was a missionary, as was Karl Isenberg, Marie Gundert's first husband, who had died young. And it was the prospect of missionary work that had led Hermann's father, Johannes Hesse, to leave his Baltic homeland.

Hermann Hesse was given the Christian name of his two grandfathers. Both men influenced him strongly—though he never actually knew his paternal grandfather, who died at the age of 94 in 1896: ". . . the best stories I ever heard as a child were those my father told us about him and Weissenstein, where he lived. Though I never saw my grandfather, his house, the town he lived in, or his garden with its maple and its green benches, yet I know Weissenstein and its neighborhood better than many towns and districts that I have actually seen. And although I had no particular enthusiasm for historical thought, and never interested myself in my ancestry, I have always felt particularly close to this wonderful man." Dr. Carl Hermann Hesse, whose forefathers came from Lübeck, was a doctor and an Imperial Russian Privy Counsellor. Monika Hunnius, his niece, described him in her memoirs as an idiosyncratic, gay, active, sociable, and pious man. At the end of his life, Hesse, who possessed a manuscript copy of his grandfather's memoirs, left us this picture of him in *Ein paar Erinnerungen an Ärzte* (*Some Memories of Doctors*): "Even at the end of his life he remained young, spirited, amusing, gentle, and relaxed. At the age of eighty-three he climbed one of his trees to saw off a branch, and fell out of it, with the saw, without suffering any harm. He founded an orphanage in his hometown, Weissenstein, drank Rhine wine on festive occasions, gave extempore speeches in verse form, observed his religious duties, and gave to the poor—he was known as 'the doctor who gives everything away' . . . Right into old age this man radiated zest for life, trust in God, authority, and love.''

Hesse's maternal grandfather, Dr. Hermann Gundert, who, like his forefathers and other members of the Gundert family, achieved high status in the annals of the Württemberg church, was also a convert to the pietism of J. A. Bengel. His conversion must have been preceded by a painful inner struggle, for this highly gifted young theologian, an admirer of Goethe, who "had copied out the piano arrangement of *The Magic Flute* with a freshly cut goose quill,'' was at the time a student of David Friedrich Strauss in the Maulbronn seminary. In *Grossväterliches (My Grandfather)*, a short memoir of his grandfather, Hesse published a poem that the nineteen-year-old Hermann Gundert had written in 1833 as a student. ''The expert will readily see that the mind this poem expresses is one influenced by Hegel and India, and familiar with Hölderlin. The writer of these successful verses wrote no more such poems. These youthful and gifted lines were written during the most agitated and uncertain period of his life, shortly before the final conversion which led the enthusiastic pantheist to devote his life from then onwards to the Indian mission.''

In 1836, Hermann Gundert arrived as a missionary on the Malabar Coast, became a pioneer of the Pietist missions to India, and spent many years working in the hot countries of the East. It was there that he met his wife, Julie Dubois, an ascetic and strict young Calvinist from a Neuchatel wine-growing family who tackled her missionary work with passionate enthusiasm. On his return from Germany, Gundert took over the direction of the Calwer publishing house. He edited missionary magazines and, thanks to his familiarity with numerous European and

11

Left: paternal grandfather, Dr. Carl Hermann Hesse. Right: maternal grandfather, Dr. Hermann Gundert.

Asiatic languages, was able to compile over the next thirty-five years the Malayalam Dictionary that to this day numbers among the basic tools of Indian linguistic research. Grandfather Gundert "was as deeply immersed in his thicket of mysteries as was his face in his white thicket of a beard, and from his eyes there flowed sometimes a universal sadness, sometimes a cheerful wisdom, a unique knowledge and a divine villainy," wrote Hesse in "The Magician's Childhood." And elsewhere he says: "In this grandfather, who died when I was sixteen, I came to know not only a wise and, despite his great learning, a very understanding old man, but also an echo, a legacy, of the remarkable combination of material frugality and spiritual splendor that characterized the Swabian milieu—in my grandfather's case, partially concealed beneath religious sensibilities and his work for the Kingdom of God, but a living thing nevertheless. The Swabian disposition, rooted in the grammar schools, the monastic seminaries, and in the famous Tübingen Stift, had held itself intact for almost two hundred years, constantly increasing and enriching itself through tradition. I refer not only to the world of Swabian presbyteries and schools, to which men of the

12

caliber of Bengel, Oetinger, and Blumhardt belonged, but to that world as a whole, which also numbers Hölderlin, Hegel, and Mörike among its sons."

The father was different. "He stood alone . . . a little apart, a suffering man and a seeker, learned and kindhearted, without guile, passionate in the service of truth . . . he was always a good and wise man . . . My father did not speak Indian dialects to my mother, but English, or a pure, clear, gentle, beautiful German of Baltic inflection. Through this way of speaking he won me to him and educated me. My father was the model that, full of admiration and zeal, I sought to imitate, too zealously, although I knew that my roots were more deeply planted on my mother's side where the soil was mysterious and rich. My mother was full of music—quite unlike my father, who could not sing at all."

Johannes Hesse's decision, after attending the famous and fashionable cathedral school in Reval, to attach himself to the very different spiritual and mental climate of Basle with the object of training himself for missionary work, was reached with great difficulty. But in time he too traveled to India, where he studied the life and speech of the Badaga and was quite soon accepted in the Mangalur seminary for the training of preachers. But his delicate constitution could not withstand the climate. In 1873, after three years in the mission field, he was forced to return to Germany, where he settled in Calw with the job of assisting Dr. Gundert in his publishing projects. In 1874 he married Dr. Gundert's daughter Marie who, since the death of her first husband, had lived in her father's house in Calw with her two sons, Theodor and Karl. Though Johannes Hesse was happy in his marriage and got on well with his father-in-law, the Swabian mentality made him uneasy. "He was a Baltic German, a Russo-German, and never, though surrounded by people—including his wife and children—whose way of speaking differed from his, did he pick up anything of it, but maintained instead his pure, refined, and beautiful High German. Though the way he spoke did not endear him to everyone who came to our house, we loved it and were proud of it. We loved it just as we loved his slim and fragile figure, his high and noble forehead, and the clear, frequently suffering look in his eyes, a look that was open and honest, a reminder of the need for decent behavior and noble bearing, a constant appeal to what was best in others.''

Marie Gundert-Hesse was small and lively, and had her French mother's lively temperament. She bore six children by her second husband, of whom two died in infancy. For forty years she kept a diary; from this record, part of which was later published by her daughter, we have a characteristic picture of this likeable woman. The diaries also contain the earliest mentions of her son Hermann who was born two years after his sister Adele, the first child. ''On Monday, July 2, 1877, after a long and difficult day, God in his goodness presented us with the long-awaited child Hermann at 6:30 p.m., a large, heavy, beautiful boy. He was immediately hungry, and he turned his bright, blue eyes towards the light, moving his head by himself. A fine example of a healthy, robust little lad.''

''I was born in the early evening of a warm July day, and it is the temperature of that day that, however unconsciously, I have all my life loved and wanted, missing it sorely when it was not to be had.''

The parental and grandparental world in which the young boy grew up was both small and spacious. The external circumstances were very simple. The pennies had to be counted, even though material possessions were accorded small value and the family knew how to live frugally. But family life in the Hesse household was rich in the qualities that ensure childhood security. ''It was,''

14

wrote Hesse to his sister Adele in 1946, "our grand-father's gentle wisdom, our mother's inexhaustible imagination and love, and our father's sensitive conscience and his familiarity with suffering, that educated us." And elsewhere: "Rays from many worlds intersected in this [the parental] house. In it people prayed, read the Bible, studied, researched into Indian philology, played music; Buddha and Lao Tse were familiar names, guests arrived from many countries bringing with them the aroma of distant places, strange traveling cases of leather and plaited bast, and the sounds of foreign languages. In it, too, the poor were fed, parties were held, scholarship and fairy stories lived cheek by jowl . . . It was a world that had the firm stamp of German and Protestant influence and yet had connections everywhere in the world; it was a complete, holy, and healthy world, united in itself. . . . It was rich and many-sided, but it was also well-ordered, precisely balanced about its center, and it belonged to us just as the air and the sunshine, the wind and the rain, belonged to us."

In the spring of 1881, Johannes Hesse was called to Basle to edit the missionary magazine. He was also required to teach German language and literature in the mission's headquarters. "Home to me was Swabia and Basle on the Rhine," wrote Hesse later. In his brief memoir of Basle he says: "From 1881 until 1886 we lived in Basle on the Müllerweg, opposite the Spalenringweg. In those days the railway line to Alsace ran between them. . . . The countryside began quite near our house. A farmyard out towards Allschwil, and a gravel pit not far from it, afforded opportunities for country games. And the enormous archery ground—how enormous it seemed to me then!—that in those days had not yet been developed, was where I hunted butterflies and we all played cowboys and Indians."

15

In the chapter in *Hermann Lauscher* called "My Child-hood," and again in the short story "Der Bettler" ("The Beggar"), Hesse provides us with a warm description of his Basle years. He tells us about the games he played and about his first day at the mission's kindergarten, of his walks to the cathedral, of childhood anxieties, and of his first clash with parental authority. With gratitude, he recalls his mother's skill as a storyteller: "Where, I wonder, do mothers acquire this cheerful and compelling art, this pictorial imagination, this inexhaustible magic? Mother, I see you still, your beautiful head inclined towards me, yourself slim, submissive, and patient; and your incomparable brown eyes!"

The young Hesse had a lively imagination, was full of energy and spirit, and the mixed inheritance of character-istics that he had received from parents and more remote ancestors soon made itself felt: ". . . the boy shows liveliness, physical robustness, and strength of will, and in addition a perceptiveness that is astounding in a four-year-old. Where will it lead?" asked his mother. On March 27, 1882, she noted in her diary that "little Hermann played truant from school and for a punishment I shut him in the spare room. Later he said, 'There's not much point in shutting me in there as I can have a nice time looking out of the window.' Recently while in bed in the early evening he sang a song whose tune and words he made up himself. When Daddy came in he said, 'I sing as beautifully as the Sirens, and am just as naughty, don't you think?'" In a letter from Johannes Hesse dated Novem-ber 14, 1883, we read that "Hermann, who is considered at the kindergarten to be the perfect child, has become extremely difficult to cope with at home. Humiliating though it would be, I am seriously thinking of putting him in a corrective establishment, or in some other house. We are too nervous, too weak, for him; our domestic life is not sufficiently disciplined and orderly. All agree that he is

16

gifted: he gazes at the moon and the clouds, improvises at long stretches on the harmonium, can draw very well with pencil or quill, sings well when he wishes, and is never at a loss for a poem.''

In 1886 Johannes Hesse rejoined the Calwer publishing house, which he was later to take charge of as successor to his father-in-law, Hermann Gundert. The family returned to Calw in July, living first with Dr. Gundert, now a widower, in the old house on the side of the hill, which also contained the publishing offices. Three years later they left this damp and unsalutary building and moved to a sunny and more comfortable house in the Ledergasse. Hesse now attended the town's preparatory school until in 1890 he was removed to the Göppingen grammar school, to prepare for the *Landexamen*. It was during these four years, his ninth to his thirteenth, that Calw became for Hesse the town that in subsequent writings appears—idealized—as Gerbersau, the most beautiful place ''between Bremen and Naples, between Vienna and Singapore.''

''I was familiar with every corner of my hometown, with the hen runs, the woods, the orchards, the workshops of the artisans, the trees, the birds, the butterflies; I could sing songs and whistle through my teeth, and many other things, too, that contribute to the quality of life . . .''

''If now,'' he wrote in 1918, ''I sit once more for a brief quarter hour on the parapet of the bridge from which as a child I dangled my fishing line a thousand times, I am powerfully gripped by an awareness of how beautiful and remarkable was the experience of possessing a place to call my own. Just once to have known in one small corner of the globe each house and every window in them, and every person behind each window! Just once to have felt inseparable from a particular corner of the world, much as a tree is bound by its roots to its own particular spot.'' And again, thirty years later, in his preface to *Gerbersau*, a book that contains all the stories that center on Calw, the writer explained: "The more old age encompasses me, and the more improbable it becomes that I shall ever again see the place where I grew up, all the more firmly implanted are the pictures of Calw and Swabia that I carry around with me. When as a writer I speak of wood, river, or meadow, the shade of a chestnut tree or the smell of a fir tree, it is the woods around Calw, its chestnuts and fir woods, that I have in mind. Throughout my books, even in those with no explicit Swabian background, there are recognizable pen-portraits of Calw's marketplace, its bridge and churches, Bischofstrasse and Ledergasse, Brühl and Hirsauer Wiesenweg; for these images and countless others served as basic models when I was young: it is not just any notion of 'Fatherland' to which I have been loyal and grateful all my life, but to these particular images; they helped to fashion my vision of the world, and they inspire me now more profoundly than they ever did when I was young."

Hesse's school memories of this period were less happy: "During the eight years I spent in junior schools I met only one teacher I could love, and to whom I now owe thanks." Other teachers he feared and hated, derided or despised. Hesse regarded school as an enemy he was entitled to fight with any weapon that came to hand. But in the case of Mr. Schmid, whom Hesse met towards the end of his schooldays as a teacher of basic Greek, things were different. Hesse discovered that for him he could feel "respect alongside the fear," and he learned that "it is possible to love and revere someone even when that person is an opponent." Greek fascinated him, and he was secretly proud to be able to learn a language "which one did not learn for financial gain or to travel the world, but just to become familiar with Socrates, Plato, and Homer."

Already, many an exercise book was filled with poems

The Hesse family: Hermann, father, Marulla, mother, Adele, and Hans (1889).

and stories. Composing rhymes, whether in German or in Latin, he found easy, and in "Curriculum Vitae" he states: "From the age of thirteen onwards I knew that I was going to be either a writer or nothing." Years later, on a walk through Tuttlingen one night, he recalled the moment of decision. "It was like this. In the Latin reader we used as twelve-year-olds there were the usual poems and stories, pieces about Frederick the Great and Eberhard im Barte, and all of them were a pleasure to read. But among all these items, there was something different, something wonderful and magical, the most beautiful thing I had ever read. It was a poem by Hölderlin called

'Die Nacht' [The Night]. Oh, those few lines, how often I read them, and how delicious and mysterious was the mixture of passion and fear aroused in me by the feeling, 'This is poetry!' 'Here is a poet!' How deep and holy and powerful was the sound in my ears as for the first time I heard the language of my parents! And, little though I then understood of their meaning, with what effect there flowed towards me from these amazing lines the magic of prophecy and the mystery of poetry!

> —the night comes,
> Full of stars, and not much concerned about us
> The wondrous shimmers there, stranger among men,
> Rising over sad and stately mountaintops.

Never again, no matter how much and with what enthusiasm I read as a youth, were words to bewitch me so totally as these did when I was a small boy.''

THE CRISES OF YOUTH

On February 1, 1890, Marie Hesse transferred her son to Göppingen. ''This was done partially for educational reasons, for I had become a difficult and ill-behaved child and my parents were no longer able to cope with me. But in addition, it was important that I should have the best possible preparation for the state examination. These exams took place throughout Württemberg in the summer of every year and were important because whoever passed them was awarded a free place in one of the theological schools and so could continue his studies on a scholarship. This was what my parents wanted for me. There were a few schools that specialized in the preparatory work for this exam and it was to one of them that I was sent. Mine was the grammar school in Göppingen, where for years old Rector Bauer had been hammering the necessary knowledge into the heads of children sent specially to him from all over Württemberg.''

Hesse studied at this school until the summer of 1891 when the exams were to be held. He lived in a children's boarding house under the strict supervision of the lady in charge, and found little to please him in this rather barren industrial town. His lessons with Bauer were productive and also humanly important. Much later, Hesse recorded an affectionate and respectful portrait of his headmaster: ''That rather weird old man, almost frightening to look at and endowed with colorful idiosyncrasies, who peered out from behind his thin greenish eyeglasses in such a glowering and melancholy way, and who kept our small and overcrowded classroom filled with smoke from his long pipe, was for some while my undisputed leader, model, knight, and revered demi-god . . . I who had always been a sensitive and anti-authoritarian pupil accustomed to fighting tooth and nail against the smallest suggestion of subservience or dependence, was now completely captivated by this mysterious old man simply because he appealed to what was best in me, and because he appeared not to notice my immaturity, bad behavior, and follies; he presupposed the best in me and took my finest efforts for granted . . . He often spoke to me in Latin, translating my name as *Chattus* . . . But what was unusual about him, and peculiar to him, was his ability not simply to detect the most highly gifted of his pupils and to nourish and strengthen their idealism, but to do justice to us as boys of a particular age who had all the faults and virtues of our age. For Bauer was not merely a respected academic: he was also a competent and highly original schoolmaster who

21

Rector Otto Bauer.

knew how to make schooling agreeable to his thirteen-year-olds.''

In his lively and graphic letters to his parents, Hesse wrote enthusiastically of this teacher, who not only had his students translate Schiller's *Wallenstein* into Latin—''that really did stretch us hard''—but also taught them to beat out its tattoo on the classroom benches, Hesse being bandmaster on these occasions. Hesse also told his parents about a short play they had staged and that he had written, and he wondered if they could produce it together when he returned home. The piece was called ''Ein Weihnachtsabend'' (''Christmas Eve''), described by its author as ''A Tragedy in One Act.'' It was a sentimental piece about a beggar child who arrives unexpectedly one Christmas Eve on the door-step of a motherless family.

The Göppingen schooldays concluded with successful completion of the exams in July 1891. In the autumn of the same year, like so many of his Gundert ancestors before him, Hesse became a student at the Maulbronn Seminary.

Württemberg's minor Evangelical theological seminaries have an educational curriculum of a type that bears
almost no comparison with anything else in Germany,
except perhaps for an inadequate one with a school like
Schulpforta, the former Meissner school for the sons of
the nobility, or with some Roman Catholic seminaries. Its
history reaches back to the Reformation. Immediately
after the Religious Peace of Augsburg, Duke Christoph,
one of the most important of the Württemberg nobles,
launched a reform of his district's church and school struc-
tures. The most consequential of his innovations was the
transformation of Württemberg's fourteen monasteries
into Protestant "monastic" schools in which young men
between the ages of fourteen and eighteen from Württemberg could be prepared as scholarship students for the
study of Evangelical theology. This edict, confirmed by
the Diet of Württemberg in 1565, yielded unsuspected
fruits, for the influence of these seminaries, even though
in the course of time they shrank to only four establishments
(Maulbronn, Schöntal, Blaubeuren, and Urach), extended
well beyond the other Württemberg schools. The particular Württemberg style of spirituality, biased though it
undoubtedly was in many respects, established itself
largely through these seminaries and then through the
University of Tübingen's seminary of Evangelical theology. Many who became famous as writers or scholars,
such as Johannes Kepler, Hölderlin, Mörike, and Robert
Mayer, received part of their education in one of these
schools. Most theologians, and the majority of teachers and
professors, but also the senior officials of the former Duke-
dom and Kingdom of Württemberg, spent their formative
years in these establishments, which then, as today, corresponded to the four higher classes of the humanistic
Gymnasium. The careful selection of students, chosen
exclusively on intellectual performance, the strength of

tradition—expressed among other ways through the simple, almost monastic way of life—and the humanist-Protestant educational ideal based on a somewhat ponderous and unfashionably strict style of teaching, gave these boarding schools their particular character, their formative influence, and their authority. It was undoubtedly a system that had its faults, but it was the strong hold on tradition and the schools' refusal to indulge in impetuous experimentation that contributed considerably to their power.

Having held Basle citizenship so far, Hesse, now fourteen, had to take out Württemberg citizenship in order to enter the Maulbronn Seminary. He was there for little more than six months. But that was enough to give his literary work a characteristic tendency that one might call his Maulbronn heritage. His story *Unterm Rad* (*The Prodigy*), published in 1906, contains Hesse's first account of his seminary and late-teen-age years. Much later he gave us a further account in *Begegnungen mit Vergangenem* (*Encounters with the Past*): "It was the period that ten years later in *The Prodigy* I tried for the first time to evoke, though even then I was still a long way from a real understanding of myself and control of my situation. In the story and person of little Hans Giebenrath and his friend Heilner I wanted to write about the crisis that took place during those years of development and in so doing liberate myself from the memory of it. In order to make good what I lacked in stature and maturity, I cast myself somewhat in the role of accuser and critic of those powers that held Giebenrath prisoner and that once very nearly captured me also, namely, school, theology, tradition, and authority. As I say, it was a premature undertaking and only partially successful . . . but . . . the book nevertheless contains a piece of life as I found it and suffered it at the time."

The beauty and fascination of Maulbronn, a former Cistercian monastery and one of the finest and best-preserved monastic buildings in Germany, is recalled in various essays and stories of later years. In *Narziss und Goldmund* (*Narcissus and Goldmund*) it is disguised as Mariabronn; and *Glasperlenspiel's* Castalia is difficult to imagine without Maulbronn as its inspiration. "It is a consoling thought that here and there in the midst of the ruins of Germany and Europe there are still such centers of new growth as these monastic schools," wrote Hesse to the Director of Maulbronn after World War II.

"The visitor to Maulbronn passes through a picturesque gateway into a large and peaceful open space. There he will see a fountain and some ancient and rather grim-looking trees. On either side stand solid stone houses. In the background is the front of the church with its Late Romanesque and uniquely beautiful vestibule, known as 'Paradise.' Astride the church's roof sits a rather strange and needle-sharp little tower which, almost incredibly, manages to support a bell. The cloister, also a fine piece of architecture, contains a charming fountain chapel and the men's refectory with its vigorous cross-vaulting. Oratory, parlatory, lay-people's refectory, abbot's quarters, and

Left: church and "Paradise," Maulbronn. Right: the Cloister Fountain, Maulbronn.

two more churches make up another massive bulk of stonework. Picturesque walls, oriels, doorways, a small garden, a millhouse, and domestic quarters surround the rather heavy-looking old buildings and make the whole seem snug and cheerful." There was something almost miraculous about the fountain chapel. "I . . . saw the fountain's three basins dancing freely in the clear shade of the vaulted room, one above the other, and the singing water fell in eight clear streams from the first basin into the second, and again in eight clear, ringing streams from the second into the gigantic third, and the vaulted roof made endless and gentle play with the living sounds, today like everyday. The fountain stood there in majestic self-sufficiency, perfect and complete, as though it were an image of the timelessness of beauty."

The fact that Hesse ran away from the seminary has led people to see the Maulbronn period too exclusively as a time of spiritual conflict. During the first few months, the opposite was the case. As numerous letters to his parents show, Hesse very soon felt at home there. His letters contain lively descriptions of daily life in Maulbronn, of the teachers, his studies, his companions, and even of the food. His grandfather in Weissenstein was also the recipient of a detailed account of a typical Maulbronn day. With twelve others, he shared a dormitory called Hellas, which he made an excuse to see himself as a Hellene. The other dormitories were Forum, Athens, Sparta, Acropolis, and Germania. They rose at 6:30 a.m. and by 6:50 they were at early morning prayers. Lessons began at 7:45, broke off at midday, and began again at 2:00 p.m. At 7:30 p.m., after supper, there was a recreation period before the day closed with evening prayers. Actual lessons occupied forty-one hours in the week but additional periods were set aside for discussion and preparation. There was little free time.

Hesse enjoyed the lessons and, with the exception of those who took him for music and physical training, he liked his teachers. "Homer is magnificent," he wrote home on one occasion. And then: "Translating Ovid into German hexameters is very enjoyable." He particularly enjoyed writing essays. "Today I had the pleasure of hearing an essay of mine, a 'Short Biographical Note,' read to the class as the best effort," he wrote proudly during his first week at Maulbronn. A little later, he wrote to say that he had had an essay returned to him with the ambiguous comment, "You have imagination." He went on to say that "he was having a difficult time with an essay called 'A Precise Characterization of Abraham on the basis of Genesis 12-15 and 21-24, with the object of showing how he was God's best choice for the foundation of the People of God chosen from among all the heathen.' It isn't going to be easy. We only have a week to do it in." He also enjoyed public readings, and to further this interest he and a few friends started a society: "There are now ten of us. We read selections from Schiller's plays, sharing the parts among ourselves; read out our own and other people's poems, criticize one another's work, etc. . . . I've promised them a paper on Goethe for next Sunday." Later they read Schiller's *Parasit* and Voss's translation of the *Aeneid.* "These evenings are always the best and most restful." He then turned to Schiller's prose works, enjoyed Klopstock's *Odes,* and asked his parents if he might be permitted to read the same writer's *Der Messias.* With a view to improving his own style, he borrowed a copy of Kurz's *Manual of German Prose* from the library.

He also wrote to his parents about a night-time brawl with one of the other students, and about the dramatic dowsing of a fire in the almshouse adjacent to the monastery. Pen sketches of his fellow students were also sent home. With a few of his companions, notably Otto Hartmann, Schall, Häcker, and Zeller, he established friendships that were to last a lifetime. "I am happy and contented! There is an atmosphere here that is just right. Best of all is the easy relationship between students and teachers . . . there is no tension here . . . and then, of course, the building itself! How magnificent it is! There is nothing more agreeable than talking in one of the cloisters with a friend about language, religion, art, and so on."

That letter was written on February 24, 1892. Three weeks later, with no apparent reason and taking neither money nor coat, Hesse ran away after lunch one day. He was not missed until afternoon lessons began, and when he failed to show up during the next few hours, search parties were despatched to comb the surrounding woods. Professor Paulus wired his parents in Calw to say, "Hermann missing since 2:00 p.m. Can you throw any light on this?" Next, the local police and the officials in neighboring villages were informed. On the late evening of the same day, Paulus told Hermann's parents that there was still no sign of him, and early next morning he wired them to say, "All possible steps taken—so far fruitlessly." Hermann did not return until towards midday, exhausted and hungry, and accompanied by a huntsman. "Thank you for such a kind letter," he wrote next day to his father; "—so you are not too displeased with your stupid dreamer who caused you so much worry. Uncle [Friedrich Gundert] will give you the details of what happened. During those twenty-three hours I wandered about in Württemberg, Baden, and Hesse. Apart from the night—8 p.m. to 4:30 a.m.—which I spent in a field at a temperature of seven degrees below freezing, I was walking all the time. Please may I give up my violin lessons, for if I don't I shall find no more pleasure in this place . . . Please love me now as before. In haste, Hermann."

28

His teachers showed him sympathy and treated him considerately. But good order required satisfaction, so the fugitive was punished with eight hours detention "for being absent without leave." On March 12, Hermann wrote to his parents telling them: "I am now in detention eating bread and water; it began at 12:30 p.m. and ends at 8:30 p.m. . . . just now I was reading Homer, a marvelous passage from the *Odyssey* . . . Things aren't too bad, though I'm terribly weak and tired, physically and mentally, but I'm gradually recovering." His letter ended with the observation that he had just read on the wall of the detention center the inscription "Karl Isenberg, May 28, 1885"—in the circumstances a consoling sight, for Karl Isenberg was his mother's first husband.

Not until March 20, when the next letter was written, do we find mention of the tensions he felt and of his depressed state of mind. "I am so tired and so indifferently disposed . . . but not ill, it's just that I'm gripped by a quite unaccustomed weakness . . . my feet are perpetually frozen while somewhere in my head a fire burns." He quoted Herwegh's song, "I should like to fade away like the sky at sunset." Partially on account of pressure from his parents, he was deserted by most of his friends. The consequent feeling of isolation caused him much suffering. After the Easter holidays, which he spent, irritable, listless, and preoccupied, in Calw, he returned to Maulbronn only to experience a worsening of his situation. Proper work became impossible. In May 1892, his father called him home, where, with a view to recovering his health, he was freed from all further studies and duties for the rest of the year.

Running away from Maulbronn, in itself little more than the impulsive reaction to stress of a sensitive and easily excitable young man, marked the onset of a period of grievous psychological turmoil which erupted now and again in the form of minor nervous breakdowns. Hesse was struggling to discover and assert himself, and to protect his identity from the inroads of the stubborn religious attitudes and traditions of his family and from the powerful complex of authority by which he saw himself surrounded. "For more than four years nobody could get what they wanted from me because everything went wrong; no school wanted to keep me and there was no subject in which I was able to persevere. Every attempt to make something useful out of me ended in failure and as often as not in scandal and humiliation, in escape or expulsion."

In May 1892, Hesse was handed over to Christoph Blumhardt, theologian and family friend, who, as his famous father's successor, had taken over the direction of the Bad Boll school, and who was also well known as an exorcist and successful faith healer. To start with, things went well. But a new crisis blew up, supposedly caused by disappointed love, and this time it led to a suicide attempt. Blumhardt gave up, and asked the boy's parents to take him away, since he could do nothing with him.

Hesse's next stop was Stetten, a school in Remstal near Stuttgart. He was given some garden work to do and was expected to help in the teaching of backward children. Outwardly, he appeared to pull himself together, and reports from Pastor Schall, the school's head, sounded hopeful. But in himself he was still wrangling with God and the world. He made it clear that he felt rejected and forsaken. His wish to be sent to a Gymnasium if he could not go to a seminary was eventually fulfilled. He left Stetten in October 1892, spent a few miserable weeks at a school in Basle, and then moved on to Bad Cannstadt to attend the Gymnasium there. But even now he only managed to hold out for just over a year. He began visiting the local bars and running up debts. But he also sat up in his garret until late at night reading Heine, Gogol, Turgenev, and Eichendorff's *Memoirs of a Good-for-Nothing*. His moods alternated between *Weltschmerz*, the tensions engendered by moral scruples, and a determination to enjoy himself. Though his year in Cannstadt ended in failure, Hesse had at least begun to work for himself. He was also fortunate to have met in Dr. Kapff a sympathetic teacher whom he was to turn to many times in the coming years.

In October 1893, Hesse was apprenticed to the Mayer Bookshop in Esslingen. Three days later he ran away. He told his father that he could summon up no enthusiasm whatsoever for the things people wanted him to do. His father received him back again and after a few months found him a position as an apprentice mechanic in Heinrich Perrot's clockmaking business.

This was the year—June 1894 to September 1895—in which Hesse succeeded in mastering himself and his worries. This we know from the few but informative letters he wrote to his friend and former teacher, Dr. Kapff. In May 1895, he wrote Kapff a somewhat self-conscious account of what had happened to him over the past few years: "Bit by bit, I'm now at last regaining peace and serenity and mental health . . . the evil times of anger, hatred, and suicidal thoughts are now behind me. But I owe to those years the gradual strengthening of the poet in me; and I have successfully survived that desperate *Sturm und Drang* period." This wide-ranging letter showed clearly that it was his writing that interested him most. He maintained that his father was too preoccupied with his own literary projects to have any time for his son's efforts. Yet he was grateful to him for many things, notably for the reading he recommended.

This was also the year in which Hesse showed signs of becoming the voracious reader that he was to remain for the rest of his life. His father's and grandfather's libraries were at his disposal. He spent all his free time reading and began to formulate a program for the study of literature. If he himself hoped "to become a decent stylist," then he must read with that in mind.

His reading included Goethe and the Romantics, Dickens and Sterne, Swift and Fielding, Cervantes and Grimmelshausen, Ibsen and Zola, and again and again his particular favorite, Korolenko. He also wrote some poems, most of them in the style of Eichendorff and Geibel. "Makuscha" is an example of these early efforts. It was written in June 1895, and it appeared a year later in the journal *Deutscher Dichterheim* as one of his first published poems. It starts:

> *In a dream the leaden sea's pale length*
> *Lay limitless beyond the vacant beach;*
> *The day was dull, the storm was spent*
> *And cloud-drifts floated overhead.*

His apprenticeship to Heinrich Perrot—a name that Hesse later gave to the discoverer of the mechanics of "the glass bead game" in the book of that name—ended after fourteen months. Hesse never regretted this brief excursion into the field of practical mechanics, but he now returned with his parents' agreement to the profession of bookseller which he had earlier and so summarily forsaken. He successfully applied for a three-year apprenticeship with the Heckenhauer Bookshop in Tübingen where he was to be trained in publishing and secondhand bookselling, as well as for work in the shop itself.

THE BOOKSELLER

Hesse moved to Tübingen on October 17, 1895. The bookshop was opposite the seminary church and not far from the Old University. He was to work in it for four years, ten to twelve hours every day, first as apprentice and then as second assistant. Work began at 7:30 a.m. and, with an hour's break at midday, ended at 7:30 p.m. Like the other apprentices, he had to pack and deliver orders, mail prospectuses, produce invoices, despatch papers and journals, and keep an eye on the stock of secondhand books. He studied the catalogues and eventually became familiar with a bookseller's method of accounting. Most of Heckenhauer's trade was in theology, philology, and law. There was room for a large stock and the bookshop had its own bookbindery.

The manager's name was Carl August Sonnewald. At first, Hesse had very little contact with him. "I have very considerable respect for him," he wrote home, adding that "he is very well educated but speaks the Swabian dialect." But the real boss was the chief clerk, Heinrich Hermes, a knowledgeable and articulate man of forty. There were also four other employees and two delivery boys. Hesse's immediate boss was a Mr. Straubing. There was no time for boredom. Hesse enjoyed himself and found the work satisfying. Unhappily, his old headaches now returned and the long hours of standing tired him so that when work was over he would return home exhausted.

Throughout his Tübingen period Hesse lived at 28 Herrenberger Strasse, just outside the old town, in a somewhat bare and desolate ground-floor room. Of his widowed landlady he said: "She's like a character from a

Tübingen.

Dickens novel, lively, catty, full to bursting with tales and stories, and yet friendly and affectionate.''

With his first paycheck he bought a plaster cast of the Hermes of Praxiteles and starting with this began to decorate his room which, when he took it over, had nothing on its walls but a large color print of King Karl of Württemberg. He ''nailed [to his wall] over a hundred pictures, sometimes large photographs, sometimes cuttings from journals and publishers' catalogues, of men that for one reason or another I admired, and I added to the collection constantly. I can still remember well how with a heavy heart I paid a rather high price for a photograph of the young Gerhart Hauptmann whose *Hannele* I had just read." He also displayed two pictures of Nietzsche and an enormous reproduction of a portrait of Chopin. "Besides these pictures, in student style I devoted the wall over the sofa to a symmetrical arrangement of tobacco pipes."

During these Tübingen years Hesse subjected himself to a rigorous program of self-education. This he did in private study during the evening hours. In November 1895, he wrote to Kapff: There are days, or at least hours, when I have a clearer and deeper insight into my hitherto rather unsuccessful life and a more profound awareness of what I wish to make of it, and this makes me feel easier than I have for a long time." In the same month he wrote to his parents: "However much I am sometimes drawn to the sources of knowledge, and however willingly I while away an occasional hour with the motley crowd in the university assembly hall, I still cannot help thinking that academic study is not ideal, but rather is circumscribed and incomplete, like everything on this earth . . . It is up to the individual to see that he learns something, becomes something, that he finds freedom, and that he reserves his interest for what is true and noble." He considered that his "period of free-thinking unbelief" was conquered, and that, even if he was unable to confess belief in the Christian God, he was nevertheless animated by a "belief in an eternal purity and power, in an ineradicable ethical world order . . . This faith proceeds from aesthetics and as such is consonant with my own inclinations."

He found himself "spiritually elevated" by Mendelssohn's *Phädon* and the Bible, his particular favorite being Genesis, then Jeremiah, Ecclesiastes, and the Psalms. The poetic passages in the Old Testament attracted him strongly, and in a letter to his parents dated October 23, 1895, he remarked that nothing had ever moved him so much as these words from the last chapter of Ecclesiastes: "the almond tree blossoms . . . and desire fails; because man goes to his eternal home, and the mourners go about the streets."

"My daily prayer is that I shall be true to my own inner world, that I don't become stunted," he wrote in a letter to Kapff, to whom he also complained in April 1896 of his loneliness. He said that for at least two or three months he had been on his own every evening and every Sunday. "Strange, that ever since my childhood I have been condemned to loneliness; she is by now an old familiar of mine. I find no friends, very probably because I'm too proud and will not go out of my way to make them. For three years now I've been accustomed to thinking alone, and singing alone."

Statements like these result from passing moods and are not to be taken literally. They contradict other statements made in letters of the same period. We know that in Tübingen Hesse met several former school friends from Göppingen and Maulbronn, that he was invited to attend the seminary, and now and again student parties. He also joined others at Professor Haering's house when the latter gave one of his traditional open evenings, and became a friend of the theology student Eberhard Goes. But he remained an outsider and tended to keep to himself. His position as an apprentice bookseller and the limited amount of free time available to him as a consequence offered little opportunity to see his older and much freer friends. Increasingly, he withdrew into his own world and concentrated on his private studies. "Every hour that I am without a piece of worthwhile reading matter strikes me as an hour lost. The wasted moments have never weighed upon me to the extent that they do now." He replaced friends and social life with the world of books and poetry, and with neither teacher nor close acquaintance he proceeded to build a world of his own: "Though the day's work is tiring, yet it arouses in me the desire to blow away

the dust and doubles the attraction of intellectual exercise
. . . It's the work I do on my own that makes life
worthwhile." He persevered in spite of handicaps; indeed, he maintained that were all his time his own he
probably would not increase the share devoted to study.

Central to this autodidact's private studies was the
reading of Goethe. Fascinated and possessed by him, for
some while he read nothing else. "Oddly enough, I have
found learning and evaluation an easier process since I
turned to Goethe and gained from him a particular
viewpoint from which to form this or that judgment."
Goethe gave him "a sense of security"; Goethe "edu-
cates"; Goethe "Teaches harmony." He enthused over
Reinecke Fuchs; Wilhelm Meister, and *Poetry and Truth*—not,
however, *Faust*—became his literary gospels. Similarly he
interested himself in Goethe's life, his letters, and his
Converstions with Eckermann; and, always with Goethe as
starting point, in Lessing, Schiller, Greek mythology,
Virgil, and Homer. "Of all German writers, it is Goethe
to whom I owe most, who occupies me most, claims my
attention, encourages me, who forces me to emulation or
opposition," Hesse confessed in his essay *Homage to
Goethe* (1946).

On October 2, 1898, having just been promoted to
bookseller's assistant, and so for the first time able to
stand on his own feet financially, he wrote to his parents:
"Apart from all the wrongs I have done you and for which
I need your forgiveness, the only thing that really troubles
me is that I have fallen into the world of commerce
because I ruined my prospects of achieving something
better. The calmer I become and the more I try to enjoy
and work hard at what I am doing, the more convinced I
become of its relative inferiority—it is after all nothing
more than buying and selling . . . when the evening
comes I turn at once from the outside to the inside of

books and systematically pursue the history of literature and the history of thought generally—studies that will, I hope, in future time be turned to good account."

It is the romantic's world that now holds him imprisoned. He reads Brentano, Eichendorff, Tieck, Schleiermacher, and Schlegel, studies their letters, and strives to familiarize himself with the history of literature. He discovers Novalis. "I consider him to be the finest of all recent German poets because he never wrote a single word that was merely decoration or rhetoric."

The autodidact in him carried Hesse ever deeper into a world of his own. He constructed for himself an aesthetic world picture, a kind of poetic pantheism, and though he told his worried parents in his letters that the Christian faith signified for him a strong and living power, it was the world of beauty in which he found faith—and that meant the world of poetry. As early as 1897 he said: "I have been convinced for a long while now that, for artists, aesthetics replaces morality." This dangerous and initially very poorly elaborated aestheticism is the intellectual background of Hesse's first poems. It dominates in *Eine Stunde hinter Mitternacht* (*An Hour behind Midnight*), as also in parts of *Hermann Lauscher,* and was only gradually shaken off in the writing of *Peter Camenzind* (1904).

Few of Hesse's early poems were preserved, but now and again a journal would accept one, and he wrote home proudly about his first small fees. His first published poem was probably "Madonna," which appeared in 1896 in the fifth number of *Deutsche Dichterheim*, a journal of poetry and criticism published from Vienna. The same journal also published other poems of his in subsequent numbers and volumes. Many of these were later reprinted in *Romantische Lieder* (*Romantic Songs*) (1899), his first collection. It seems, however, that he submitted many more poems than were printed. Evidence of this comes from the journal's editorial comment on rejected work, where on one occasion we read: "H-n H-e in T-n: He doesn't seem to like his fellow men! In twenty lines two references to 'disgust' at the 'masses'! . . . A pity about the two attractive concluding verses: they deserved something better."

Characteristic of Hesse's style of thought in those days are the comments on Chopin which he made to his parents in September 1897 after they had quite understandably expressed unhappiness with a poem he wrote about the composer. "What Wagner was to Nietzsche, Chopin is to me—or even more so. Everything important in my intellectual and spiritual life is in harmony with his warm and living melodies, with his piquant, lascivious, and nervous harmonies, with the rare intimacy of his music. I must constantly admire his refinement and reserve, and his complete sovereignty. Everything about him is noble even if much is also degenerate."

Writing to Kapff, Hesse described his work with intentional irony as "lyrical trinkets and pious ejaculations." But that he was nothing if not serious in his attempts to write poetry can be seen from the trouble he took to familiarize himself with the rules of language and with prose and poetry generally. "The study of the laws of linguistic euphony, and the puzzles of interior rhythm that escape all precise inquiry, proceeding on to those mysterious areas where, murmuring darkly in the eternal emergence of things, one finds what I should like to call 'the rules of pitch,' is a particularly satisfying occupation."

His first collection of poems appeared in 1899 under the imprint of the Dresden publisher, E. Pierson, to whom many a young poet had entrusted his first offerings, more or less paying the production costs themselves. This was *Romantic Songs*. Only a small edition was printed. Hesse began it with a quotation from Novalis:

> *Look, the stranger is here who feels exiled*
> *From the same country as you, the hours have become*

> Sad for him; the joyful day
> Ended early for him.

The first poem is called "An die Schönheit" ("To Beauty"), and its third verse runs:

> Danger and strife sank
> In the dark flow of time,
> My loneliness vaulted
> By distance and expanse.
> Green and gold and sky dissolve;
> Above the banks of my afflicted
> Soul lay the home for which I long.

Images and sounds of tired sadness, heaviness of spirit, longing, and homesickness dominate in all these poems. They are the dreams of a lonely and sensitive heart that feels uneasy in this world and so indulges in accusation and rejection. The form of the poems shows definite ability and above all a highly developed ear for euphony and rhythm;* and though it is not difficult to point to the influences he reflects, a few of the poems and some verses show an original approach peculiar to Hesse. In a letter dated December 2, 1898, to his mother, who had read the manuscript and here and there offered criticisms, Hesse wrote the following: "The title itself is a type of personal confession. I see it as the end of a period and believe that in my future work there will be no further sign of it. The

---

*In the original German the poem reads:

> Tänze und Gefahren sanken
> In den dunklen Fluss der Zeit,
> Ohne Nähen, ohne Schranken
> Wölbt sich meine Einsamkeit.
> Grün und Gold und Himmel schwand;
> Überm Ufer meiner kranken
> Seele liegt mein Heimwehland.

manuscript was finished early in the year and since then I have become more solitary, more peaceful, and clearer in myself . . . the process of editing, the selection of one poem rather than another, I think I managed to liberate from personal prejudices. The book is not supposed to be a *mélange* but something complete in itself, a sequence of sounds and variations on the same romantic theme.''

"An Hour behind Midnight" was also included in this collection. He gave this title to his second book, a series of nine short, prose pieces that was printed by Drugulin and published in 1899 by Eugen Diederichs in Leipzig. Hesse was in touch with Helene Voigt, the publisher's wife, in connection with his poems, and he probably owed the acceptance of his second manuscript largely to her recommendation. Diederichs suggested an edition of 600. He had no great hopes of commercial success, but he was convinced of the collection's literary merit. He said, "I don't think we shall sell even 600 copies but I'm hoping that people will notice the book if only because of the fine production and that in this way we shall compensate for the author's unknown name.''

In a preface to a subsequent edition of this book (1940) Hesse wrote: "Regarding the title of my first prose collection, though its significance was clear enough to me, few readers made anything of it. What I wanted to suggest through this title was the kingdom in which I lived, the dreamland of my working hours and days that lay mysteriously anywhere between time and space. Originally, the title was to have been *Eine Meile hinter Mitternacht* (*A Mile behind Midnight*), but that was too similar to the title of the fairy story *Drei Meilen hinter Weihnachten* (*Three Miles behind Christmas*). So I thought of *An Hour behind Midnight* . . . I had created for myself in these prose studies an artist's dream world, an island of beauty, and

41

the writing that came from it was a retreat from the storms and stresses of the daytime into the night, dreams, solitude . . .''

Rilke wrote highly of the book in a review: ''In its best passages it is compelling and strange. Its reverence is sincere and profound. Its love is great and all its sentiments devout: it stands on the borders of art . . .'' Hesse admitted the influence of Maeterlinck that Wilhelm von Scholz detected. He also conceded that he was at that time in danger of pursuing a somewhat sickly form of ''introversion.''

During his last two years in Tübingen, Hesse joined a group of friends who called themselves the ''Petit Cénacle.'' One of them was Ludwig Finckh, a law student and a ''gifted and extremely wealthy but unusually humble and lovable person. Literature interested him, but art was his first love . . . some of his verses and sketches show a rare degree of gentleness, sweetness, and feeling . . .'' Carlo Hamelehle, the second member of the group, ''is full of questions but has no answers; he is a lawyer and philosopher''; and there was Oskar Rupp, ''a quiet, hard-working, well-balanced person; he listens more than he speaks and one misses him when he is not there. The four of us meet over some beer for one evening nearly every week from 7:30 until 11:00, not noisily, as the students do, but joyfully nevertheless.'' Later, the group took in Schöning and Otto Erich Faber. Hesse was fondest of Finckh who was soon to give up the law and turn instead to medicine.

On August 31, 1899, Sonnewald wrote in Hesse's final report that ''he had always been hard-working, loyal, and honest,'' and that he had acquired ''a thorough knowledge,'' and that ''his modest bearing and his upright character . . . would be great assets to him in later life.'' Hesse left Tübingen, but before returning to Calw, from where he was to start a new job, he spent a few happy and

42

The "Petit Cénacle": Otto Erich Faber, Ludwig Finckh, Hermann Hesse, Carlo Hamelehle, Oskar Rupp.

relaxed days with his "Petit Cénacle" friends in nearby Kirchheim at the foot of the Swabian Alps. There he got to know "Lulu," young Julie Hellmann, the niece of a local tavern keeper. The group made a great fuss over her, and Hesse observed that instead of taking his leave and moving onwards he was becoming hourly more involved in the relationships that were developing. Later, Ludwig Finckh described their holiday, and Hesse preserved the Kirchheim episode in the Lulu chapter of *Hermann Lauscher* and also in a few poems. It had been a mixture of happiness and melancholy.

"My only wish was to return to Basle; it seemed that there was something waiting for me there and I did my best to secure a position in Basle as an assistant in a bookshop. I was successful and arrived in Basle in the autumn of 1899 with Nietzsche's works (so far as they were then published) and a framed copy of Böcklin's *Toteninsel* in the suitcase that also held all my other possessions. Being no longer a child, I felt I need have nothing to do with the Basle of former days, with the mission house or its atmosphere; I had already published a small volume of poetry, had read Schopenhauer, and was

43

enthusiastic about Nietzsche. Basle was for me above all things the town of Nietzsche, Jacob Burkhardt, and Arnold Böcklin.''

So Hesse chose a town with historical associations and one that also had strong connections with the fine arts, thereby rejecting such centers of contemporary literary life as Berlin and Munich. This very conscious decision, a somewhat surprising one for a poet to have made, had a decisive effect on his future.

There was little change as far as his job was concerned. Once again, he was back behind the bookshop counter doing the various jobs he had turned his hand to in Tübingen. He was now one of six employees in the Reich'schen Buchhandlung.

Though he had come to know Basle quite well as a child, now as a young man the town opened up a new world for him and enlarged his horizons considerably. Parental connections gave him access to some of Basle's most influential families.

". . . on one of the first Sundays I diffidently sought out the house of the historian and archivist R. Wackernagel, to whom my father had given me an introduction. He lived behind the Württemberger Hof on the Brunngässli. He made me welcome, and shortly afterwards I was received with equal kindness by Jakob Wackernagel in the Gartengasse. Soon, in addition to my work and my colleagues there, I had excellent contacts with several Basle families, all of which were in some way connected with the University. In this way I came to know many of the younger people who belonged to the town's learned society. Those I saw most often were Joël, Wölfflin, Mez, Bertholet, and Johannes Haller.

"In these circles everybody lived under the influence of a man who for several decades had been the intellectual mentor and cultural arbiter of Basle's learned society. His

44

name was Jacob Burckhardt and he died only a few years ago. Though I, too, had read him—*The Civilization of the Renaissance* in Tübingen, and *Constantine* in Basle—I was too deeply fascinated by Nietzsche to allow much of a foothold for Burckhardt's direct influence. All the stronger was the indirect influence he exerted on me. Receptive and anxious to learn, I moved within a circle of people whose knowledge and interests, reading and travels, style of thought, understanding of history, and conversation, were influenced and molded by no one as powerfully as they were by Jacob Burckhardt.''

Towards the end of his life, Hesse stated that the three most powerful and constant influences on him had been "the Christian and almost totally un-nationalistic spirit" of his parental home, his "reading of the great Chinese writers,'' and by no means least "the influence of the only historian I was ever devoted to and whom I could feel trust and respect for: Jacob Burckhardt.''

Hesse enjoyed his visits to archivist Wackernagel's house and there, as well as during the musical evenings in the La Roche household, he became familiar with this particular form of refined society and with the living spirit of its cultural inheritance. Basle also opened his eyes to the fine arts and to beauty in its more sensuous manifestations. He visited the cathedral almost daily and spent hours in the art galleries and museums. In a letter to his parents he said: "Being surrounded by works of art has done me untold good—it is as though a large part of me has been asleep all this time and is now being awakened by a flash of sunlight in the eyes . . . Recent years of exclusive concentration on bookwork and literary pursuits have given me a strong thirst for the things the senses find beautiful . . . My table and bed are piled high with art journals and reproductions of Renaissance paintings, and I have spent all day cutting them out and mounting them.''

Arnold Böcklin's work attracted him particularly, and again and again he visited the art museum's Böcklin Room. Böcklin's *Vita Somnium Breve* impressed him most. "It is as satisfying to my very modern sense of color as it is to the old-fashioned pleasure I take in allegory."

Hesse was gradually establishing a more stable relationship with reality. He was gaining in self-confidence. On September 12,1899, he wrote to his friend Ludwig Finckh: "After many sacrifices along the way we have found our goal. I am working here in Basle with an antiquarian bookseller, selling valuable old books. But I am also about to write things that no man has written before. The romantic period has fled and Lulu is now no more than a sacred star in the heavens. I have even found friends, and you must come down and visit us in Basle and Riehen, visit the Wackernagels, the La Roches, stand on the Rhine Bridge and listen to the river rushing past."

"I find myself well-placed and living a full and exciting life between profession, private work, and social life," he told his parents. At the end of his first year he wrote to them saying: "My inner life and literary plans have gradually acquired a degree of clarity and a sense of direction that make any incidental difficulties seem trifling. Though there are still things to worry about, I have never experienced a year so rich in thought, self-knowledge, decision, and achievement as the one that has just gone . . . my chief concern after so much haste and disruption is to achieve a sense of youthfulness and well-being and to spring-clean and expose to the sunlight my somewhat fusty and distorted earlier existence. This I need more than I can say."

The experience of art and history was accompanied by a fresh experience of nature. From now on, nature and tradition become the two forces that accompany him through life. Hesse traveled throughout Switzerland,

46

chiefly in the area round the Vierwaldstätter Lake. On Sundays he would often visit the Jura Mountains, or the southern regions of the Black Forest. More ambitious expeditions took him in summer and winter into the Bernese Oberland to Grindelwald and to the Gotthard. He was particularly fond of boating on the lake near Vitznau and Brunnen. He would lie for hours in the bottom of the boat, daydreaming and watching the clouds and the butterflies. "All day long I cruise around in the boat, out in the open and into the inlets. A boat, a cigar for when I'm idling, a volume of Plato, and some fishing gear—that's how I relax."

In March 1901 he went to Italy. "It was my first visit to Italy, and I had looked forward to it and saved for it for a long time. First I went via Milan to Florence, spent a few weeks in Tuscany, visited Bologna and Ravenna, and after a short stay in Padua reached Venice . . . I had to live very cheaply, being entirely dependent on the money I had with me. As long as the money lasted I could stay, and in fact I managed to squeeze out another week. The more frugally I lived the happier I was, for I got to know Venice a lot better that way than the apparently more fortunate gondoliers."

Hesse devoted his evenings to literature, chiefly to the history of art and to his own writing. Now and again, short essays, poems, and reviews appeared in print. He made contact with Hans Trog, an editor on the *Allgemeinen Schweizer Zeitung*. In 1901 the publishing house of the bookshop where he worked issued his *Hinterlassenen Schriften und Gedichte von Hermann Lauscher* (*Surviving Poems and Prose of Hermann Lauscher*). It was a modest little volume of only eighty-three pages and a very small edition was printed. Hesse himself appeared in the guise of editor. In 1907 a new edition was published, its title now shortened to *Hermann Lauscher*, and its contents extended by the inclusion of two other sections, "Lulu" and "Schlaflose Nächte" ("Sleepless Nights"). This book constituted a considerable advance on *An Hour behind Midnight*. Hesse later described it as "an attempt to capture for myself a small piece of world and reality and to escape the dangers of an isolation that was due in part to shyness and in part to arrogance." Many of the characteristics of form, theme, and tone that were to come to full bloom in later works were present here for the first time. The book is rightly regarded as a private statement of the author, for, apart from the description of his Basle childhood mentioned earlier, it also contains, as its most important piece, the *Tagebuch 1900* (*Journal for 1900*). Beginning on April 7, and continuing on into the autumn of the same year, these journal entries provide an unvarnished account of Hesse's unstable intellectual and spiritual condition at that time; they witness also to passionate self-questioning and to the growth of his ability as a writer.

Meanwhile, Hesse's life was still affected by emotional ups and downs, even though these were now milder and more easily controlled than before. He fell in love with Elizabeth, the proud daughter of the La Roche family, but shyly kept his distance; he drank in the Basle taverns with a group known as the "Klub der Entgleisten" ("The Failures' Club"); he dreamed sadly of the transience of things and was plagued by hypersensitivity. He would like to rid himself of his phlegmatic nature, "blow it like a bubble into the sky." But autumnal moods still dominated. He dreamed of the beautiful lady he had seen playing Chopin's E-flat major nocturne; continued to revel in the clutches of *Weltschmerz*, and reminded himself of the "great change, the uncertainty of the ground we build on, death, and the countless wearisome paths that we have so vainly pursued." The cult of aestheticism and the tendency to flirt with irony and cynicism were still there. But Hesse was sure enough that "if anywhere, the joy and meaning of life lie in forward progression, in the evermore conscious clarification and penetration of the essence and laws of beauty."

The journal contains a few passages of considerable formal beauty and it demonstrates Hesse's ability to write successful descriptions of the natural world. His language has become more sensuous and the reader can feel how assiduously he cultivates this quality. "Could one call oneself a linguistic *pointilliste?*" he asks himself. "What is blue-green? What is pearl-blue? How does one express the unobtrusive dominance of, say, yellow, cobalt blue, violet?—for in this unobtrusive dominance lies the enchanting secret of a particular mood." In *Drei Zeichnungen* (*Three Sketches*), lyrical prose pictures written in 1901 by the Vierwaldstätter Lake but not published until years later, Hesse's beloved butterflies and clouds are already in evidence as particularly favorite subjects.

Even when he was an old man, it was Hesse's custom to make handwritten copies of certain poems and to distribute these to a small circle of friends. He always wrote as though for the individual, never for the crowd, and placed little value on publicity. The first signs of this exclusivity date from the Basle period. "Of two poems completed this year only one was published for a wider public," he wrote in a letter to his closest relatives, "the other [he is referring to the poem "Notturni"] was distributed in manuscript form to a very small number of friends, well-wishers of mine . . . this intimate style of communication . . . gives me the advantage of being able to preserve my poems from the mechanics of publication, the speculations of the trade, and the prating of the press. I then know that they will only be read by the well-disposed."

C

In July 1900, Hesse had to present himself to the Lörrach district's army-selection board. But he was turned down on account of serious near-sightedness, and was put on the army reserve list. This, of course, suited Hesse very well, as military service didn't attract him in the least. But his weak eyes were to plague him throughout his life, and he frequently suffered the headaches and neuralgia of which his father was also a lifelong victim.

To have more time for his writing, Hesse resigned his position in the Reich'schen Bookshop and in September 1901, after a lengthy stay in Calw, joined the staff of Herr Wattenwyl's antiquarian bookshop in the Pfluggässlein. The old-fashioned and ponderously slow style of working in a bookshop owned by a man who was more bibliophile than businessman did not bother him in the least. In Julius Baur, his immediate boss, he found a man who was not only one of the best-informed representatives of his trade, but also one of "the purest, most kind-hearted, most genuine, and most lovable of men" that he was ever to meet. As Hesse later confirmed in *Beschwörungen* (*Evocations*), Vasudeva, the ferryman in *Siddhartha,* is based on Julius Baur.

Hesse's monthly salary was not more than 100 francs. To have survived on such a salary would have been impossible, but he managed to make ends meet and to live free from debt with the help of the fees he received for his published poems and for the articles he wrote for various papers and journals about his Italian journey. In March 1902, after much initial hesitation, he accepted the attractive offer of the post of assistant in Leipzig's museum of book production. "The greater freedom of movement and life in the . . . now so familiar Switzerland," seemed to him not to outweigh the advantages of the Leipzig post.

In the same year, Hesse's third book was published. It was a large collection of poems and it appeared under the imprint of the Grote'schen Verlagsbuchhandlung in Ber-

lin in its *Neue Deutsche Lyriker* (*New German Poets*) series.
There were about 200 poems, arranged according to
theme. The section headings were "Von Wanderungen"
("From Journeyings"), "Buch der Liebe" ("Book of
Life"), "Irrweg" ("Wrong Way"), "An die Schönheit"
("To Beauty"), "Süden" ("South"), and "Zum Frieden"
("To Peace"). Busse wrote in his Foreword that in
Hermann Hesse contemporary literature's neo-
Romanticism had found one of its strongest and most
striking talents, and that however much one might find
related passages in Lenau or Verlaine, Hesse most certainly had a style of his own. Among the most remarkable
poems of this early collection was "Ravenna," subsequently set to music by Schoeck.

> *I, too, have been in Ravenna.*
> *It is a little dead city*
> *That has churches and a good many ruins.*
> *You can read about it in books.*
>
> *You walk back through it and look around you:*
> *The streets are so muddy and damp, and so*
> *Dumbstruck for a thousand years,*
> *And moss and grass, everywhere.*
>
> *That is what old songs are like—*
> *You listen to them, and nobody laughs*
> *And everybody draws back into*
> *His own time till night falls into him.*

The book was dedicated to his mother. But she was not to
witness its publication, for on April 24, she died after a
long and painful illness. "Unless I'm very much mis-
taken," wrote Hesse a year later, "I have our dear
mother, whose living spirit I constantly feel around me, to
thank for what is best in me."

One day, very much to his surprise, Hesse received a

letter from the publisher Samuel Fischer. It was a request that Hesse submit work to him. The Swiss writer Paul Ilg had drawn the attention of this influential publisher of modern poetry to *Hermann Lauscher.* Replying on February 2, 1903, Hesse explained: "I hardly need to stress that what I write is always a very personal attempt to express intimate matters in modern form, and thus is unlikely to enjoy any appreciable degree of success as a book. I do not write much and when I do it is only as a consequence of highly personal necessity." He said that he had nothing he could send immediately, but he promised him "a small prose composition" which he had been working on for several years. This was *Peter Camenzind,* a piece that was first published in the *Neue Rundschau* (1903), a journal, and later (1904) in book form. *Peter Camenzind* brought its author immediate fame and marked the beginning of his reputation as a great writer.

With this story about Camenzind, the farmer's boy from Nimikon, Hesse overcame the depressing melancholy that had marked the *Lauscher* era. It was as though a younger, healthier, more robust writer were at work. Though its naturalism and naïveté are somewhat overdone, and its critique of its times, society, and civilization is very poorly founded, his vigorous descriptions of nature—mountains, clouds, the sea—the powerful rhythm of his language, and the ethos of the book as a whole, are all very effective and contributed considerably to the great success Hesse had with it.

Speaking of Camenzind, Hesse said: "My intention, as is now known, was to familiarize modern man with the overflowing and silent life of nature. I wanted to teach him to listen to the earth's heartbeat, to participate in the life of nature, and not to overlook in the press of his own little destiny that we are not gods, not creatures of our own making, but children, parts of the earth and of the cosmic whole. I wanted to remind people that, like the songs of the poet and our night-time dreams, rivers, seas, drifting clouds, and storms are symbols and bearers of our yearnings, yearnings that embrace the earth and the heavens and whose object is the undiluted certainty of citizenship and the immortality of all living things . . .

"But I also wanted to teach people to find the springs of joy and the waters of life through affectionate familiarity with nature: I wanted to preach the art of observation, walking, and enjoying, of finding pleasure in what is at hand. In compelling and forceful language I wanted to make you open your ears to what the mountains and the green islands have to say; I wanted to force you to see what an immensely varied and busy life there is there, daily blooming and bubbling over, outside your homes and towns. I wanted to make you ashamed of knowing more about wars, fashion, gossip, literature, and the arts than you do about the spring who displays her vigorous life outside your towns, or about the river that flows beneath your bridges, or the woods and the meadows that your railways pass through. I wanted to tell you what a golden chain of unforgettable pleasures I, a solitary person ill at ease in this world, had found, and I desired that you, who are perhaps happier people than me, should discover even greater joys."

In 1951, in a letter to a student who was studying *Peter Camenzind*, Hesse wrote: "Camenzind tries to get back to nature, away from society and the world; he repeats in a minor form Rousseau's half-courageous, half-sentimental revolt, and in this way becomes a writer.

"But, and this is the distinguishing characteristic of this early piece of writing, he does not belong to the boy scouts or any of the other youth organizations: on the contrary, for nowhere would he fit in worse than with these ingenuous and noisily self-conscious groups that

53

either play guitars around the campfire or spend the night in argument. A man is not at his best as a member of an association, a participant in a conspiracy, or a voice in a choir. Instead of community, cameraderie, and classification, he seeks the opposite; he does not want the path of the many but—obstinately—only his own path; he does not want to run with the pack and adapt himself, but to reflect nature and world in his own soul, experiencing them in fresh images. He is not made for life in the collective but is a solitary king in a dream world of his own creation.

"In this, it seems to me, there lies the continuous thread that runs through all my work. I do not now share Camenzind's somewhat cranky eremitical attitudes; I have not run away from contemporary problems in the course of my development as a writer, and despite the assertions of my political critics to the contrary, I have never shut myself up in an ivory tower. The truth is that I was primarily concerned not with the State, society, or the Church, but with the individual man, the personality, the unique, free individual."

In April 1903, Hesse accepted an invitation to visit Florence and so found himself in Italy for the second time. One of his traveling companions was Maria Bernoulli, who came from Basle of a family well-known for its pursuit of scholarship. She ran a photography studio in Basle with her sister. Hesse was nine years her senior. They married in the summer of 1904, and thanks to royalties received from the sale of *Peter Camenzind*, Hesse was now able to give up his job and pursue a full-time literary career. "Now at last, after so many troubles and sacrifices, I had achieved my goal: impossible though it had once appeared, I was now a writer and had won my long and arduous battle with the world. The bitterness of my school years and of the subsequent years in which I was growing

54

to maturity and when I so often came close to shipwreck, was now forgotten, something to laugh about—even the relatives and friends who earlier had not known what to make of me now smiled on me approvingly. I had conquered, and no matter how stupid some action of mine might now be, others found it charming; and I was more than a little pleased with myself. Only now did I realize in what horrifying isolation, asceticism, and danger I had lived, year after year. The recognition had done me good and I began to become a satisfied man.''

THE BODENSEE YEARS

The fairy tale *Iris,* one of Hesse's most charming stories, bears the dedication ''For Mia.'' It was published in 1918, which means that he had dedicated it to his wife at a time when their marriage was already over. The story tells of a young boy called Anselm who loved the iris more than any other flower in his mother's garden. He often dreamed about the flower, and when he was older he met a girl who bore the same name: ''She was older than he would have liked in a wife. She had an outlook all her own, and he saw that it would be difficult to live together with her while also pursuing his scholarly ambitions, as she was quite uninterested in them. Neither was she very strong or healthy and so could not, for instance, tolerate much social life or go to parties. She preferred to live in solitary peace with flowers, music, and a book, and would wait to see if anyone would visit her. For the rest, she was happy to let the world go by. Sometimes she was so delicate and sensitive that anything unaccustomed would hurt her and easily reduce her to tears. Then suddenly, peace-

In Gaienhofen with his first wife, Maria, née Bernoulli.

fully and delicately, she would glow again with private joy, and whoever observed it would sense how difficult it would be to give anything to this strange and beautiful woman, or to mean anything to her.''

Hugo Ball interpreted this fairy tale in his biography of Hesse; Iris was his wife, Maria, the woman who was so much like his mother.

The wedding was celebrated in Basle. By common agreement they decided to live in the country and ''lead a simple, natural, unurban, unfashionable, and country life. The thoughts and ideals that led us to this decision had as strong a connection with the outlook of Ruskin and Morris as with that of Tolstoy . . . To start with, we looked for a house in one of the pretty villages around Basle. Then as a result of my first visit to Emil Strauss in Emmishofen, the Bodensee area (Lake Constance) was also drawn into our range of choice. Finally, while I was staying with my father and sisters at Calw at work on *The Prodigy,* my wife discovered the village of Gaienhofen on the Untersee, and there in this village was an empty farmhouse on a small, quiet square opposite the church. I agreed at once, and so we rented our farmhouse for 150 marks a year, which we thought cheap . . . the only cosy thing about that house was the fine old porcelain stove which was heated from the kitchen. Water had to be drawn from a nearby well, and nowhere in the district was there either gas or electricity. It was not easy to get to the village, or to leave it; apart from the steamboat, and that didn't sail very often (if there was ice or a storm, not at all), there was only a horse-drawn mail coach which, after a journey of several hours and with long stops at every intervening village, would take one to a railway station. But the house was just what we wanted, a charming and remote nest, with no noise, but with pure air, a lake, and a wood.''

They took only half the house, the other half, a haybarn and a stable, being reserved by the farmer for his own use. The living quarters of the timber-framed building consisted of a kitchen and two small rooms on the ground floor. On the next floor was Hesse's book-lined study with a high desk and another writing desk specially made in Munich. From this room there was a view of the lake.

"What made this house special and dear to me was something no later house could provide: it was our first! It was the first refuge of my young marriage, the first real workplace of my chosen profession. Here for the first time I had the feeling of being settled, and precisely for that reason also, now and again, that of being imprisoned by regulations and domestic arrangements; here for the first time I permitted myself the pleasant dream of being able to create and earn such a thing as a place to call my own, and in a house of my own choice, too.''

57

Evening on the Bodensee (Untersee).

Insight into the daily life of those days, and its problems, is afforded not so much by the volumes of stories that resulted from the Gaienhofen years as by a few sketches published here and there, though not in book form until 1926, under the title *Bilderbuch* (*Picture Book*). The relevant section of this book is called "Bodensee." Not long married and only just settled, Hesse already began to feel uneasy about his comfortable life and to consider himself in the land of the Philistines. There seemed to be something dubious about his newly found security; having achieved something, he found there was still more he wanted, and there were times when he would take up coat, hat, and stick, and, with no particular aim in view, walk out into the night.

In one of the *Picture Book* pieces he describes an evening in their Gaienhofen house, and tells how he sat at his work table reading a translation of Ossian from an old quarto volume while in the next room his wife played the piano. "She is playing short, agitated pieces by Schumann. The gentle tones of the music and the reddish candlelight stream into the room together through the wide-open door." But then she turns to Chopin: "Gentle, shy tones, blurred and dreamy rhythms, wonderfully elegant figures, the chords exciting, as though distorted, and no longer possible to distinguish harmony from dissonance. Everything pushed to the limits, everything uncertain, like one walking in the night, and in the middle of it all, like a thin stream, a sweet, gentle, childlike melody . . . It is pleasant to sit at a strong table, a sound roof over one's head, a dependable wine to drink, a large and well-filled lamp burning, and in the next room, door open, a woman playing the piano, selections from Chopin, and candlelight . . . But suddenly I wonder: Are you really happy?"

Feelings and moods of this type are deeply embedded in Hesse's nature. They do not become really troublesome

59

until later on in the Gaienhofen period, but already at the outset they prod him gently. Yet Hesse knows very well that ". . . had I not worked today, and made some small forward progress, then tomorrow or the day after, this whole day would sink irretrievably into the abyss to join all those other buried days which I have nothing to remember by." The urge to profit from every moment never left him. Though he always liked to assess and reflect upon his feelings, dreams, and hopes, the hard reality of his life was constant activity. He remained a steadfast worker until the day he died.

They lived in the old farmhouse for three years. Their first child, Bruno, was born there on December 9, 1905, and many of Hesse's poems and stories were written there. But then they had to leave the house, and since they failed to find anything else that suited them, Hesse, in matters of this type always very dependent on his wife, decided to buy a piece of land and build for himself. "Perhaps there was nothing more behind this decision than the domestic urge, though that had never been very strong in either of us . . . or was there something of the peasant ideal at the back of it? In fact, however, I was never very sure about my peasant ideals, not even in those days, but derived from Tolstoy and Jeremias Gotthelf, nourished by the movement from town to land then quite strong in Germany, where it was underpinned by moral and artistic considerations, this attractive but only vaguely formulated article of faith came to life within us . . .

"We selected a spot quite a long way outside the village; it had an uninterrupted view across the Untersee. One could see the Swiss shore, the Reichenau, the cathedral tower in Constance, and in the background, the distant mountains. The house was larger and more comfortable than its predecessor and provided space for children, maid, guest . . .

On the terrace of his house in Gaienhofen. Scissor-cut by Otto Blümel.

"Almost more important than the house was the garden. I had never had a garden of my own and it followed naturally from my country convictions that I should lay it out, plant it, and care for it myself; and so I did. I . . . planted trees, including chestnuts, a lime tree, a catalpa, a beechtree, and any number of fruit bushes and trees . . . And nearby I planted a bed of dahlias, and I made a long avenue on either side of which a few hundred enormous sunflowers grew, while at their feet there blossomed many thousands of small flowers in every shade of red and yellow."

Close by, Ludwig Finckh, his Tübingen friend, set up his medical practice. Finckh's first house was burned to the ground not long after completion, and while its owner was on his honeymoon. Hesse helped him to rebuild it, and the two men amused themselves with boat and fishing rods on the lake and along its banks. They met and became friends with other writers whose homes were nearby, among them Emmanuel von Bodman and Wilhelm von Scholz. And in ever-increasing numbers, Hesse's fellow writers came to visit him, often from afar. Stefan Zweig came (but hit his head so hard while passing through the door that he had to lie down for quarter of an hour before he was able to speak); and Martin Lang, with whom Hesse wrote poems, caught butterflies, drank and talked, and worked in the garden; and then Wilhelm Schussen and Bruno Frank. Wilhelm Schäfer, Emil Strauss, Jakob Schaffner, Alfons Paquet, and several other writers and poets joined the growing circle of friends, colleagues, and acquaintances. One day the aging Christian Wagner turned up, an ordinary peasant who wrote quite extraordinary poems and yet who could only inappropriately be called a "peasant poet": "To those who have ears to hear, the solitary eccentric was not merely a poet from whom one now and again might expect something good, but also a representative of a particular spirit, a particular type of German nature and thought at the moment accorded small respect but whose fruits lie in the future. He belongs to that group of men whose best and most succinct statement of belief is to be found in Adalbert Stifter's preface to *Bunte Steine*."

Hesse's most successful friendships were with musicians and painters. To this day, Höri, a charming stretch of country by the Untersee, exerts a strong attraction on painters. Max Bucherer, whom Hesse had already met in Basle, lived for a while in Gaienhofen, and when he left two other painters, Otto Blümel and Ludwig Renner rented the vacated house. Hesse toured northern Italy with Fritz Widmann, and with Hans Sturzenegger, whose studio in Belair near Schaffhausen was the scene of many a lively party, he traveled to India. He also came to know Albert Welti, Cuno Amiet, and Gustav Gamper; and later, Ernst Morgenthaler became an important member of Hesse's closest circle of artist friends.

Musicians were also frequent guests. Music had always

1907.

been important to Hesse. At the age of nine, his parents
had given him his first violin, an instrument he had
enjoyed playing ever since. His wife was an accomplished
pianist. At the very beginning of their Gaienhofen days,
they had met Dr. Alfred Schlenker. "He was a dentist in
Constance and was one of a group of youthfully idealistic,
open, high-minded, art-hungry people who lived in that
agreeable little town. But music and its encouragement
were his first loves. I have much to thank him for, but
most of all for the hours we spent with the then twenty-
year-old Othmar Schoeck. Schlenker was a friend of his,
and he soon came to know other musicians of our

generation, notably Fritz Brun and Volkmar Andreae."
Schlenker, who was an excellent pianist and also a composer, asked Hesse to write the libretto for an opera.
"The result was *Die Flüchtlinge* (*The Fugitives*), dashed off
with impudent ignorance of the problems involved in a
fashion that only the impatience of youth and the stimulat-
ing atmosphere of a lively friendship make possible."

Othmar Schoeck, with whom Hesse quickly made
friends and who often visited him in Gaienhofen, was "for
many years the doorkeeper and guardian of a world that
without him I could never have gotten to know so closely
and so directly . . . In gratitude for all that he had given
me I wrote for him in the first years of our friendship the
text of a romantic opera, and I no more regret having done
so than I lament the fact that he was unable to make use of
it.

". . . what I liked about him particularly, and what
made him so valuable to me, was the way in which his
nature combined opposing factors—extrovert robustness
and sensitivity, an understanding for the most naïve of
pleasures together with an understanding for the things of
the mind, his many-sided and by no means untroubled
personality, the sensual man in harmony or even at odds
with the intellectual."

Soon Hesse deepened his acquaintance with the conductors Volkmar Andreae and Fritz Brun, with the
Lieder-singer Ilona Durigo, and later with Busoni and
Edwin Fischer. Schoeck, Fischer, Andreae, and many
others set poems of his to music. In Zurich, Hesse went to
concerts and operas, and in April 1911 he went with
Andreae to Milan to hear the first performance of the
latter's B-minor mass. "My friendships and meetings with
composers, conductors, virtuosi, and singers," Hesse
later recalled, "formed an indispensable part of my musical life . . ." Music strongly influenced the content, lan-

guage, and sound of his poetry. "As a lyricist at heart, the need for a melody is ultimately stronger in me than that for weighty subject matter," Hesse wrote to Theodor Heuss in 1910.

Though Hesse made the acquaintance of many poets and writers in the course of his life, the number of his friends from the worlds of art and music was greater. He sought them out and relaxed with them more readily.

Hesse's success and fame grew fast during the Gaien-hofen years. In the autumn of 1904 he was awarded the Bauernfeld prize, which brought him 1000 crowns. The Swabian Schiller Society elected him an associate member; the first Hesse Society was formed, and as he ironically (but not without pride) informed his father and sisters, his name was included in Mayer's small encyclopedia.

Peter Camenzind, enthusiastically reviewed and often reprinted, was followed by *The Prodigy,* most of it written during a long visit to Calw (1903/4) but completed in Gaienhofen and published in book form by Samuel Fischer in 1906 after first appearing in two journals, the *Neue Zürcher Zeitung* and *Kunstwart.* This book, too, went through many impressions and quickly took its place on the list of novels about schooldays and youth that were then fashionable reading matter. It has affinities with Emil Strauss's *Freund Hein,* Friedrich Huch's *Mao,* and even, up to a point, Robert Musil's *Young Torless.*

During the next two years, *Diesseits* (*This World*) and *Nachbarn* (*Neighbors*), two collections of short stories, were published, and *Umwege* (*Deviations*), the third volume in this group, was added in 1912. Most of the stories in these books had already appeared previously in journals. Several were subsequently revised.

It is not so much the events of which these stories treat, or the treatments themselves, interesting though both are, that make them memorable, but rather the melodious and

65

impressionistically modulated style in which they are written. They unfold memories of youthful experiences with nostalgia and gentle irony. Whether the subject is the intricate development of his emotional life—the awakening love in child and youth; the first encounter with death—or a description of some aspect of the countryside, these stories always faithfully reflect the author's experience of life. "Die Marmorsäge" ("The Marble Saw") and "Heumond" ("July Moon"), "Der Lateinschule" ("Grammar School"), "In der alten Sonne" ("In the Old Sun"), or "Schön ist die Jugend" ("An Ode to Youth"), to mention just a few of the titles, are the result, like all the others, too, of observations made within a simple, rural world. It is a world of schoolmasters and craftsmen observed and represented according to life, without false pathos or cheap sentimentality.

Wider in scope but less successful and timeless than many of the short stories and sketches is his novel *Gertrud* (*Gertrude*), which first appeared in 1909 in Velhagen and Klasing's *Monatsheften*. Told in the first person, it is the life story of Kuhn, a musician crippled by a childhood accident. He loses the woman he loves to a friend, but after the latter's early death maintains a platonic friendship with her. This is the only book Hesse wrote that he ever called a novel. Its reception was mixed. "Along with unreserved praise, the fickleness of the press, which will call a writer a genius until it tires of him and declares him an idiot, was also strongly in evidence," wrote Hesse to Conrad Haussmann. He went on to say: "It may well be true that Gertrude does not emerge very clearly as a character: to me she was more of a symbol than a character, and at the same time the stimulus behind Kuhn's development.

Unterwegs (*On the Way*) is a piece of heady nature lyricism and contains a carefully selected group of poems about spring, summer, solitude, sleepless nights, and

66

nostalgia for lost youth. The book was designed by Hesse's friend Otto Blümel, who decorated it attractively in the style of the time. Only a small, numbered edition was published.

> *Those of us born in July*
> *Love the smell of white jasmine,*
> *We wander in the flowering garden*
> *Quiet, and lost in leaden dreams.*

> *Our brother is the scarlet poppy*
> *Burning in flickering red shivers*
> *In the cornfields and on the hot walls*
> *And then the wind blows away its petals.*

Wholly dependent upon his writing, Hesse was obliged for financial reasons to increase the quantity of his contributions to papers and journals. Over the years he wrote a considerable number of book reviews and articles on literature generally. These pieces, whose quantity testifies to Hesse's wide reading and rigorous work schedule, appeared over such a long period of time and in so many different journals that they have not yet been collected and so are difficult to assess. Hesse always remained an attentive and critical observer of contemporary literature, and through his reviews and articles exercised a stronger influence on the literary life of his times than one might at first suspect. He was never a party to literary rows and polemics. If he disliked a book, his usual custom was not to review it. Before the First World War, his individual and group reviews appeared predominantly in *Propyläen*, *Schwabenspiegel*, *Rheinlanden*, and *März*. For *Propyläen*, a literary bi-weekly edited by Eduard Engels and published for subscribers to the *Münchener Zeitung*, Hesse wrote quite extensive monthly articles on "Recent Narrative

Literature." In his introductory article to this series, in which he said that his object was "not to criticize, not to weigh individual words, but to select and introduce what was best," he wrote with surprising optimism of the narrative literature of his day, though he was critical of the popular pastime of pigeon-holing a piece of writing almost before the ink was dry, ascribing it immediately to this school or that tendency. "How am I helped by the knowledge that this or that writer is a symbolist, a nature writer, a disciple of Maeterlinck, or a friend of Stefan George?!"

Hesse also contributed to *Die Rheinland* (for a short time he was also its literary editor), a monthly journal of "German Art and Style" edited by his friend Wilhelm Schäfer. Though primarily concerned with the fine arts, it also published original literary contributions.

But of all these journals, the most important was *März*. Hesse not only wrote for this journal from time to time but edited it jointly with Ludwig Thoma, Albert Langen, and Kurt Aram (Hans Fischer's pseudonym). Devoted to German *Kultur*, this twice-monthly journal was launched and named by Albert Langen, the imaginative publisher who in 1896 had already founded another journal, *Simplicissimus*. He called on Hesse in Gaienhofen in 1905 and invited his help. Hesse agreed, and not long afterwards, having been joined by Ludwig Thoma, *März* was started in Munich. Hesse was not directly involved in the journal's political section, but was concerned exclusively with its literary coverage. However, he was in full sympathy with *März's* liberal and democratic political attitudes, including of course its campaigns for peace and non-isolationism. An incisive opposition journal, he told his father, was necessary and helpful. The first number appeared in 1907. His name as joint editor appeared in the journal until December 1912. In 1911 it became a weekly and in its last years, during the First World War, it was managed by Theodor Heuss. *März* published many of Hesse's best occasional writings and although Hesse was later to regard his change from the world of art into that of moral and didactic literature with misgivings—"a service performed without full inner conviction but undertaken for reasons of conscience"—it was a duty he took very seriously at the time. The contributions were selected with a fine feeling for quality, and younger and unknown poets were given their chance along with the established writers. Now and again, he included translations of foreign authors—Selma Lagerlöf, Strindberg, and Shaw among them. "Whereas many a slim volume of poetry has long since sunk beneath the waves, with the exception of a few purely topical pieces, the narrative literature published in *März* has preserved its appeal," observed Hannsludwig Geiger in his memoirs.

Editorial work often took Hesse to Munich, where he struck up a close acquaintance with Ludwig Thoma. Reinhold Geheeb, editor of *Simplicissimus,* a journal for which Hesse wrote numerous poems and essays, became a close friend, and through his work on *März,* the Swabian politician Conrad Haussmann also joined his circle of close friends. In a letter to Haussmann dated October 2, 1909, Hesse wrote: "I am glad and comforted to know that you want to remain a friend of mine. For years now, since my nerves got the better of me and I ceased to have any great affection for life, I have always been surprised and pleased to find that in spite of this now and again someone healthier, more competent, and happier than me likes me and accepts me as I am."

In addition to his editorial work and his activity as a literary critic, Hesse was also engaged in the preparation of new editions of the poets and the publication of anthologies. These projects started during the years immediately before the outbreak of war and in the course of time became increasingly important. Hesse never regarded them as a mere ancillary occupation, and they constituted a considerable part of his life's work. Among the first of such projects was a selection from the poems of Mörike, the poet to whom Hesse felt particularly close and whose works he frequently promoted in the columns of *März*. The first of the anthologies, jointly edited by himself, Emil Strauss, and Martin Lang, was a selection of German folk songs published under the title *Lindenbaum*. Other similar volumes followed in quick succession. The *Lieder deutscher Dichter* contained "A Selection from Classic German Lyric Writing from Paul Gerhardt to Friedrich Hebbel." *Der Zauberbrunnen (The Magic Fountain)* brought together poems from the Romantics, and another anthology was devoted to "Selected Readings from German Prose and Lyrical Poetry of the Classical and Romantic Periods." Editions of Jean Paul, Eichendorff, and Christian Wagner were also added. In the year 1913 alone six books edited by Hesse were published. The unusual knowledge of German literature Hesse had acquired in the course of constant reading over many years was being put to good use in a type of work that suited him well, and he regarded the process of preserving and handing down as one of the noblest duties of the thinking man.

Before the outbreak of war it became almost habitual for Hesse and a few friends to visit northern Italy in the spring of every year: "Between Locarno and Verona, Basle and Brig, Florence and Perugia, there are few places that I have not passed through in dusty boots two or three times." Poor health, particularly his eye afflictions, often obliged him to attend health resorts—Wartemberg, Badenweiler, and once a log cabin on Monte Verita in Ascona. In summer, and sometimes in winter also, he visited the Swiss Alps, being accompanied on these occasions by his wife, a keen mountaineer and skier. But as more and more lectures and public readings were pressed upon him, travel increasingly became a matter of business rather than pleasure. When in the late autumn of 1903 he was invited for the first time to give a public reading, he told the President of the Zurich Literary Society that he had never been in a club's rooms, and that as a very reserved "poet of the woods and the countryside" his sole experience of such an activity was the one occasion on which he had read something to a small group of friends. But only a few years later the newly successful writer found it almost impossible to turn down such invitations. Two or three times each year, partly glad of a change and partly irritated by the need to forsake his country retreat for a few weeks, he visited various German and Swiss towns to present himself to his readers through his own readings. Sometimes such journeys took him to Vienna, Prague, Strasbourg, and Saarbrücken. They usually ended in dejection and bad conscience, for at heart Hesse knew very well that such activity was against his basic nature. "I have never liked appearing in public, and it was always disagreeable to find oneself in a milieu where one was a 'name' and a 'commodity.' I could never have too much privacy, and for this reason I have never attended an assembly of prominent people."

In 1909, while on one of these tours, Hesse visited the seventy-eight-year-old Wilhelm Raabe in Brunswick. Raabe was a poet for whom Hesse had great affection and respect. Later he wrote an account of the visit: "Slim and tall, this gentle and impressive figure received me in a long bathrobe and as though from a great height his old wrinkled head looked down towards me, quizzical and wise, endearing and kind. Yet his was the countenance of a fox—sly, cragged, mysterious; the aged face of a wise man, ironical without malice, knowing but good-hearted,

71

possessing the cleverness of age and yet ageless—aided in this respect by an upright physical stance; a face that was quite different from my grandfather's, and yet related to it, of the same period, of the same austere maturity, of almost the same dignity and nobility, a face overspread and softened by the many-sided play of knowing and experienced humor.''

In a letter dated April 2, 1910, to Otto Hartmann, a friend from his Maulbronn days, Hesse complained of the increasing volume of work: "Every day a pile of letters, annually over 300 books to review, and in addition the work on *März*, various journeys, illness, wife and children, and finally the garden—much that I should like to do never gets done." And in a letter to his sister Marulla written on Christmas day of the same year, he wrote: "For several years now I have been so familiar with states of depression, and feelings of isolation and lack of courage, that I now prefer anything else, even pain."

The problems connected with the Gaienhofen way of life, having first emerged in the Bodensee writings of the initial years, although not apparent in the other work of that period, began now like a worm in an apple to eat away at an outwardly successful career.

"Im Nebel" ("In the Mist") is the name of a frequently quoted poem, written as early as 1906, that expresses his inner feelings. The last verse runs:

> *Strange, to wander in the mist!*
> *To live is to be alone.*
> *No man knows the other,*
> *Each of us is on his own.*

Hesse became increasingly convinced that life in Gaienhofen was exhausting him mentally. He was besieged by restlessness and doubt and felt himself a stranger in his own house. Wife and children—Heiner was born in 1909 and a third son, Martin, in 1911—did not compensate, and the once settled country life became a torture. He traveled with increasing frequency: "The world outside is so vast."

"As a young man I had imagined adulthood to be something quite different from what I actually found. Now life is once more a process of waiting, asking, and restlessness, of longing rather than fulfillment. The lime-tree blossom smells delicious, and the hikers, tourists, children, and young couples all seem to respond to a common law, appear all of them to know very well what they are supposed to be doing. I alone appear not to know . . . My lot is to follow my inner voice even when I fail to recognize its meaning and its goal, and even when it leads me ever farther away from the paths of joy into the dark and the partially known."

Hesse decided to travel to India. "With practiced impudence, modern psychologists call that 'flight,' and of course it was that, too. But it was also an attempt to step back from myself and discover what was happening." There was nothing unusual at that time about going to India. Indeed, it had become quite a popular undertaking. Melchior Lechter, Waldemar Bonsels, and Hermann Graf Keyserling had also gone there and, as Hesse was to do, had written books about their visits. But for Hesse India meant something more. It had been his mother's home-land, the country in which his father and grandfather had worked, just as it was the homeland of those little dancing idols that used to stare out from his grandfather's cabinet and that featured in so many of the fanciful young boy's dreams.

Together with the painter Hans Sturzenegger, Hesse set out in September 1911, traveled through northern Italy to Genoa and from there took the steam packet that brought them without intermediate stops to Ceylon.

From Colombo he wrote to Haussmann: "This is our first landing since Genoa. Ceylon is just like something from the Arabian Nights—hot, colorful, and narcotic in effect, like opium. The cool of the evenings here we should call the heat of the summer at home. The sun is blinding and the Singalese have the gentle smile of children . . ." In his *Erinnerungen an Indien* (*Memories of India*) he tells us: "In Penang we encountered the turbulent life of an Asiatic town for the first time, and for the first time saw the Indian Ocean glittering among the countless coral islands, and observed with astonishment the colorful life of the alleys of the Hindu, Chinese, and Malayan quarters. The alleyways perpetually full of milling, motley crowds, at night a sea of candlelight, motionless coconut palms mirrored in the water, shy and naked children, fishermen in primeval boats."

From Singapore they traveled in a Dutch boat to southern Sumatra and on from there in a Chinese paddle steamer up the Batang-Hari to Palembang. Language troubles and poor health prevented Hesse from getting to know the country and its people as well as he would have liked, and eventually they obliged him to forego his original plan to spend some time in India and to visit Malabar. "I have achieved my main object which was to observe tropical scenery and the Asiatic way of life, and I must be satisfied with that."

Somewhat disappointed by the Indians and the Malays, he was astonished by the impression of "unlimited strength and future" made upon him by the Chinese. On the return journey, a few days before they were due to embark and leave for good, he climbed Pidurutalagala, Ceylon's highest mountain. "The primeval landscape I found there affected me more strongly than anything I had seen in India. The palm trees and the birds of paradise, the rice fields, and the temples of the richer coastal towns, the valleys of the tropical lowlands exuding fertility, all that, and even the primeval forest, was beautiful and fascinating but always strange and weird, remote and separate. But up here in the cold air and swirling clouds I understood at least how totally we and our civilization are rooted in the rawer and poorer lands. Full of longing and driven by dark and grateful anticipations of homecoming, we travel southwards and eastwards and find the gifts of nature spread before us in abundance and rich luxuriousness; we find the homely, simple, childlike peoples of paradise. But we ourselves don't fit in at all, we feel foreign and out of place; we lost paradise a long time ago and the new one we want to possess and build is not to be found on the equator or among the warm seas of the East but lies within us and within our own northern future."

Ten years later, Hesse admitted that this journey, which had been a flight from Europe, had not brought him the inner liberation or the spiritual encounter with the true India that he had hoped for.

"I was not destined to find India and China by traveling there on ships and trains, but would have to locate all the magic bridges myself. I would also have to cease looking for the redemption of Europe in those quarters; I would have to cease making my heart the seat of hostile feelings towards Europe and instead learn to make the real Europe and the real East my own, in my own heart, and that lasted many years: years of suffering, restlessness, war, and despair."

It became clear to Hesse on his return from India that life in Gaienhofen could not go on. "It was beautiful and instructive but ultimately it would be a form of slavery. It was fine to play the peasant—so long as it was a game; but the joy went when instead it became a matter of habit and duty," he wrote later, consciously avoiding one of the worst problems, namely the trouble his marriage was in.

But the question was, where to go to next. In March 1912, he embarked on another lecture tour, this time to Vienna, Prague, Brunn, and Dresden. "The main purpose of this trip is to have a look at Hellerau near Dresden as a possible place for us to live. Alternatively, we think of Zurich (but that would be too expensive), Berne, and Munich," he wrote in a letter dated February 11, 1912. In a resigned mood, he wrote to Haussmann: "I can't move to Swabia as my wife doesn't want to go there. It's her point of view I consider first. She wants the children to have Swiss nationality. It's all the same to me, since I have the feeling that I won't put down roots anywhere: at least wife and children might as well attempt to do so. My relationship with my family began a long while ago to become nothing more than concern to bring in enough money to care for them . . .

"I have no wish to spoil my memories of Württemberg by making it my place of work: childhood and the Black Forest are my most sacred possessions and I shall not endanger them . . ."

They finally decided on Berne, and in the house that had formerly belonged to Albert Welti, the painter and friend who had recently died, they found just what they wanted. This move did not mean flight or emigration from Germany, however much later critics were always to maintain the contrary. Though Switzerland's political stance suited Hesse a lot better than Germany's pre-war nationalism, there was no political motivation whatsoever in their departure from Gaienhofen. "Southwestern Germany and northern Switzerland are home to me, and that the area is crossed by various national borders is something that I have often enough been made aware of, in small and in big things, but deep down I have never been able to regard these borders as natural things. Home for me lay to either side of the Upper Rhine, no matter whether the area was known as Switzerland, Baden, or Württemberg.''

THE FIRST WORLD WAR

In September 1912, Hesse and his family transferred to their new house in the Melchenbühlweg on the edge of Berne.

"House and garden were not very different from the description in *Das Haus der Träume* [*The House of Dreams*], a fragment of a novel I wrote in memory of Albert Welti, one of whose most remarkable paintings bore that name." A few months after they had settled into the new house, Hesse wrote to Haussmann: "I like Berne; if things start to go better with me, this will be a good place to live. There is no literary life, nor much in the way of art; but there's good music and some agreeable musicians, a beautiful town, peaceful and unobtrusive people—slow to make friends but thereafter, let us hope, faithful ones; in short, not the best of places, but solid, and quite the opposite of Munich."

In the guise of "Herrensitz Rosshalde," the new house was made the scene of "an allegorical novel in which the sickness and death of a lovable little boy represent the withering and death of a marriage." This story, originally a poetical account of the difficulties in his own marriage, was published in Velhagen & Klasings *Monatsheften* in 1913, and then a year later in book form. In the drawing E. R. Weiss did for the title page there is a reproduction of a painting by Johannes Veraguth that was used as a symbolic representation of this piece of writing. It consists of three figures sitting next to one another, but without any sug-

Hesse, his wife, and Heiner, their second son.

gestion of contact. "The man bowed and buried in hopeless thought, the woman yielding, waiting, joyless, the child bright and cheerful, playing among the flowers . . ."

When the book was published, Hesse wrote to his father: "The novel gave me a lot of trouble and work, and represents, at least for the time being, a departure from the most difficult problem I have ever had to face. For the unhappy marriage that the book is about has nothing to do with an unfortunate choice but is concerned with the deeper problem of the 'artist's marriage' in general, with the question whether an artist or thinker, a man who doesn't just want to live from instinct but primarily to observe and portray life as objectively as he can, is in any way capable of marriage. My book contains no answer but it does quite clearly set out my attitude towards the problem; a matter is concluded there that I hope to resolve differently in my own life . . ."

Hesse reread *Rosshalde* after a gap of twenty-six years and found that it had withstood the test of time. "With this book I reached as high as I was ever to get in terms of literary ability. I can see now that the war served a good purpose in so dramatically interrupting my development: instead of allowing me to become a master of form, it introduced me to a complex of problems that mere aesthetics could not cope with.''

The *Drei Geschichten aus dem Leben Knulps* (*Three Stories from the Life of Knulp*), which also originated in pre-war days, are concerned with former and less wearisome themes. The first of them, "Vorfrühling" ("Before the Spring"), first appeared in 1908 in *Neue Rundschau* and was not published in book form until 1915 when it was included in Fischer's *Library of Contemporary Fiction.*

Knulp is a descendant of Eichendorff's Taugenichts, a vagabond for whom everything goes wrong, a misfit who cannot settle down in the ordered world of commercial life. But behind the childlike and infectiously gay Knulp a second Knulp lies concealed, a lonely, homeless person, condemned to wander from place to place, nowhere able to put down roots. Freedom from the bonds that tie others down can only be bought by foregoing bourgeois happiness, family, and domesticity. And so, figuratively and implicitly, this story, too, is concerned with the artist's dilemma, with the tension between the productive world of commerce and the apparently useless and purposeless existence of the poet and the painter.

As Knulp, exhausted and close to death, wanders aimlessly in a dense snowstorm through his native woods, God appears to him. Knulp begins to argue with him about the pointlessness of life. "Look," God said, "I could only have used you as you are. In my name you have wandered from place to place, bringing the complacent a twinge of longing for freedom. In my name, you have done stupid things and allowed others to deride you; in you I have myself been derided, and in you also, loved.

79

For you are my child, and my brother, and a part of me; and you have tasted nothing, suffered nothing, that I have not experienced with you.''

Mention must also be made of another story written at this time, namely, "Im Presselschen Gartenhaus" ("In the Garden House at Pressel"), published in Westermann's *Monatsheften* in 1914. The impression of simplicity and assurance created by this story about Mörike, Waiblinger, and Hölderlin, Tübingen and the little garden house on the Osterberg to which the young theology students take the ailing poet, can easily lead one to overlook the high degree of artistic ability Hesse achieved in it. One thinks not only of the historical correctness of the atmosphere he evokes, of the remarkable degree of perception with which he characterizes the three utterly different Swabian poets, but primarily—and it is apparent only after close inspection of the narrative—of the powerful symbolic value he gives to ostensibly unimportant processes, and how he makes the straightforward into the significant. Hesse is using quite familiar historical material as a vehicle for his own thoughts on the nature of the poet and on the creation of poetry.

By the time World War I broke out, Hesse had already lived in Switzerland two years. He did not attempt to escape his duty as a German citizen but went to the German consulate in Berne and volunteered for military service. He was turned down, but a little later was assigned by the German embassy in Berne to the Prisoners of War Welfare Organization.

Whereas most poets in the belligerent countries, particularly in the first few weeks, indulged in tirades of hate, Hesse, not having fallen prey to the war psychosis, published in the November 3, 1914, issue of the *Neue Zürcher Zeitung* his now famous essay "O Freunde, nicht diese

Töne! ("Oh My Friends, Not These Sounds!"). Deeply upset by what was happening, he opposed the madness of nationalism and appealed to humanity and reason. Now more than ever, he wrote, it was necessary to recall the spirit in which the best German thinkers and poets lived, and to urge upon all men the virtues of justice, moderation, decency, and love for one another that the spirit implied: ". . . the elimination of war remains our noblest aim and the ultimate consequence of Western Christian civilization. . . . That life is worth living is the essential message and assurance of all art, even if all life's eulogists still have to die. That love is superior to hate, and sympathy to anger, that peace is more noble than war, are convictions that this wretched world war must impress upon us more firmly than we have ever felt them before." He is shocked by the "brutality with which all spiritual values beyond political and military affairs are nullified and spat upon."

"I, too, was once obliged to cast away my whole contemplative philosophy and offer myself to the cares of the day, and if necessary bleed myself to death in so doing. That was when the war came, and for nearly ten years I saw protest against the war, against the raw, bloodsoaking stupidity of man, against those 'intellectuals' who preached in favor of war, as a duty and a harsh necessity." Hesse belonged with the dwindling number of German poets who, from the start, determinedly opposed chauvinism and barbarity, and called for peace. But the result was alienation and hate. The German press called him a "traitor" and a "wretch"; and in a frequently reprinted article, the *Kölner Tagblatt* said: "Like a knight of the woeful countenance, shirker Hesse wanders away, a man without a fatherland, a man who inwardly long ago shook the dust of this homely earth from his boots." Among the

81

D

few who stood by him were Conrad Haussmann, Theodor Heuss, and Hermann Missenharter. The *Kölner Tagblatt's* smear article hurt him deeply: he never forgot it.

Hesse had almost no contact at all with Switzerland's German emigrés, who—Rene Schickele, Leonhard Frank, or the Zurich group of Dadaists, for example—shared an attitude similar to the *Kölner Tagblatt's*. He became increasingly solitary, joined none of the literary groups, and lived more or less incognito. He did, however, gain the friendship and respect of Romain Rolland.

Hesse was tireless in his work for the prisoners of war, and he viewed this service as one he was morally obliged to offer. "Every life stands beneath its own star, but mine was not of the heroic, patriotic, or military type; it was not required of me to worship and fight for that star, but rather the opposite: my task was to defend the private and individual life threatened by mechanization, by war, by the State, or by the ideals of the masses. I was not unaware that there is often more courage attached to the unheroic and straight-forwardly human approach than to the heroic."

From 1915 until the beginning of 1919, under the auspices of the Prisoners of War Welfare Organization, Hesse, and the zoologist Professor Richard Woltereck directed the Berne Book Center for German Prisoners of War. Its function was to provide German prisoners in France and in America, as well as those interned in Switzerland, with books and small libraries. As the official funds made available for this work were soon exhausted, the Center's performance depended largely on the activity of its two directors. In countless letters, Hesse begged books from colleagues and friends, libraries and publishers. "Of course, it's not a question of humanitarianism alone, but a political and educational one, for the moral dangers of imprisonment are considerable," wrote

Hesse in one of these letters (to Schmidtbonn, June 30, 1916). Thousands of books, sometimes small camp libraries, were amassed, packed, and despatched to the German prison camps in France. "The misery that now calls to one from every corner of the world is so terrible that I want to do everything I can to help from my humble position."

Because not enough books were presented, and because many of them were unsuitable for prisoners, Hesse started and anonymously edited a paper for war prisoners under the auspices of the neutral Berne office *"Pro captivis."* It was called *The Sunday Messenger for German War Prisoners,* and every two weeks for three years many thousands of copies of this paper were despatched to France, England, Russia, and Italy. For eighteen months Hesse also edited, with Woltereck, *The German Internees' Newspaper,* which was published by the Prisoners of War Welfare Organization in Berne. He even issued his own little series of twenty-two books from the Book Center Publishing House created for the purpose. "Stories by Emil Strauss, by the Mann brothers, by Gottfried Keller, and by myself, simply but decently produced as presents for the prisoners, who were crying out in their tens of thousands for reading matter . . ."

In addition to the severe distress Hesse experienced on account of the war, and the exhausting work in the Book Center, he was beset by grievous personal troubles: the dangerous illness of his youngest child, his father's death in 1916, the crisis in his marriage, and finally the outbreak of an emotional disturbance in his wife that made it necessary for her to spend some time in a mental home. In a volume of poetry that appeared at that time under the title *Musik des Einsamen (Music of a Solitary),* there is a poem called "Der Ausgestossene" ("The Outcast") that contains the lines:

Years without grace,
Storms at every turn,
No place to call one's own,

Just error and false trails!
God's hand bears hard
Upon my soul.

The beginning of 1916 found him so disturbed in body and mind, so spiritually depressed, that he had to interrupt his prisoners' welfare work. Gaining nothing from a rest in Locarno and Brunnen, Hesse underwent psychoanalysis in the Sonnmatt private clinic in Lucerne. There, with the help of Dr. Josef Bernhard Lang, a student of Jung who quickly became a trusted friend, and through his own intensive study of the writings of Freud and Jung, Hesse succeeded in clearing the blockage and in controlling the conflicts that had pursued him since youth. Between June and November 1916, he attended about sixty sessions with Dr. Lang but, as Ball has rightly pointed out, these were more psychotherapeutic conversations between friends than psychoanalytical treatment in the strict sense. The treatment considerably enlarged Hesse's outlook and persuaded him to follow new paths in a fresh approach to his own development as man and poet. Though we should not exaggerate the significance of psychoanalysis in Hesse's writing, it remains a fact that his acquaintance with Dr. Lang and his familiarity with the works of Jung contributed much to a clarification of his own world picture. In his essay "Künstler und Psychoanalyse" ("The Artist and Psychoanalysis"), Hesse wrote: "Whoever with proper seriousness has gone a little way along the path of analysis in search of spiritual first causes from among his memories, dreams, and associations, reaps the lasting profit that might be called the possession of the

84

'inner relationship to the subconscious.' He experiences a warmer, more fruitful, and more ardent exchange between the conscious and the subconscious; his gain in this is clarity about many things that otherwise remain beneath the threshhold and are enacted only in unnoticed dreams.

"The end of the war coincided with the completion of a change in me and with the peak of those sufferings I had successfully to withstand. These were sufferings that had nothing to do with the war or with the fate of the world, nor even with the fall of Germany—which those of us who lived abroad had anyway been expecting with certainty for the last two years. I was entirely wrapped up in myself and my own fate, though occasionally I did strongly suspect that my case had to do with everything that is inhuman. I found in myself all the war and blood lust in the world, and also all its frivolity, its pleasure-seeking, and its cowardice; first I had to lose my self-respect, and then my self-contempt; my task was quite simply to endure to the end my glance into chaos in the hope, sometimes fading, sometimes expectant, of finding nature and innocence on the other side. Anyone who is truly alive and conscious travels this narrow path through the desert once in his life, if not more often. To discuss it with those who have not done so would be a waste of time."

Blick ins Chaos (*Glance into Chaos*) is the title of a collection of three essays written in those years. *Zarathustras Wiederkehr* (*Zarathustra's Return*) and *Sinclairs Notizbuch* (*Sinclair's Notebook*) are the titles of two other books containing writings from the same period, a period that became known as the "Sinclair period," this being the pseudonym under which *Demian* was published in 1919. *Demian* is the most important and significant of Hesse's books to stem from this period of upheaval, change, and fresh beginnings. Like some of the fairy stories—*Iris,* or *Der schwere Weg* (*The Difficult Path*)—

85

Demian, written in Berne in the space of a few months, is a product of the psychoanalysis he had undergone.

Demian tells the story of a young boy, Emil Sinclair, who through meeting Max Demian, his "Demon"—the name came to Hesse in a dream—frees himself from his childhood and in debate with Demian discovers his own limitless interior world. With the help of Pistorius, modeled on Dr. Lang, he is able to regulate and master what he discovers, and finally by learning to relinquish, and ultimately no longer to need, his dominant dream image—an intense longing for his mother—he finds the way to freedom and personal responsibility. All this happens in dreams and images, with the result that the inner, symbolic world is brought into the open and he discovers his true personality. "I have always been and still am a seeker, but I no longer do my seeking among the stars or in books. I am beginning to hear the lessons which whisper in my blood. Mine is not a pleasant story, it does not possess the gentle harmony of invented tales; like the lives of all men who have given up trying to deceive themselves, it is a mixture of nonsense and chaos, madness and dreams.

"The life of every man is a way to himself, an attempt at a way, the suggestion of a path. No man has ever been utterly himself, yet every man strives to be so . . . There are many who never become human . . . Yet each one represents an attempt on the part of nature to create a human being. We enjoy a common origin in our mothers; we all come from the same pit. But each individual, who is himself an experimental throw from the depths, strives towards his own goal. We can understand each other; but each person is able to interpret himself to himself alone."

Becoming conscious of oneself leads to self-knowledge, and thus one step higher within Hesse's autobiographical writing. *Demian* is an attempt to interpret himself to himself. Through total honesty he is able to discover himself and the way appropriate to him and to affirm this way as his own destiny. Guilt is not to be sought in others but in oneself. Man is autonomous: He is responsible for his own actions.

Through *Peter Camenzind* and the music of his earlier writings, Hesse had enchanted a large number of readers who had been young at the turn of the century. But with *Demian* he attracted a new generation of readers, the homecomers from a lost war, the young people of the Twenties. The movement that the book set in motion was vigorous and enduring. Its bold and unequivocal declarations were passionately discussed. Though *Demian,* more so than his other works, may be the prisoner of the period in which it was written, it nevertheless fulfilled its function by arousing a large number of people from complacency. In his Introduction to the first American edition of *Demian* (1947), Thomas Mann wrote: "The electrifying influence exercised on a whole generation just after the First World War by *Demian,* from the pen of a certain mysterious Sinclair, is unforgettable. With uncanny accuracy this poetic work struck the nerve of the times and called forth grateful rapture from a whole youthful generation who believed that an interpreter of their innermost life had risen from their own midst—whereas it was a man already forty-two years old who gave them what they sought."

"Only the ideas that we really *live* have any value," we read in *Demian. Zarathustra's Return* is based on this theme. Written in January 1919 in the course of three days and nights, it was a solemn appeal to the youth of his times. It was written "under the pressure of world events" and in a state of the most severe "distress and tension." Like *Demian,* it appeared anonymously. Hesse was well aware of the hate and scorn young people had "for everything that appeared to them old-fashioned, out of date, or impressionistic," and he reckoned that his name, too, would be such an item of scorn. But his wish to make honest contact with them led him to put his own name to the second edition. Hesse was also recognized, by Eduard Korrodi, as the author of *Demian,* with the result that subsequent editions of this book also bore his name. This led him to return the "Fontane Prize" that had been awarded to the fictitious "Emil Sinclair."

In spite of what one might think, *Zarathustra's Return* is not homage to Nietzsche the philosopher and poet "but certainly to Nietzsche the man. Since the lamentable failure of German intellectual integrity during the war, he seemed to me more and more to be the last representative of a German spirit, a German courage, a German manliness, that appeared to have died out among our own thinkers."

"Few people perceive their destiny. Few people live their lives. Learn to live your lives! Learn to perceive your destiny!" Zarathustra appeals to youth. "You must learn to be yourselves . . . You should forget how to be others, to be nothing at all, to imitate foreign voices and to take foreign faces for your own . . .

"Don't stand around begging for the mercy of world history, you who have so recently sung Germany's praises for the good of the world; don't stand in the road like punished schoolchildren whining for the sympathy of passers by! If you can't bear poverty, then die! If you can't govern yourselves without an emperor and victorious generals, then subject yourselves to foreign rule! But, I implore you, don't forget the shame of it completely!"

The sovereignty of the free individual is set against the enticements of the collective. That the absolutizing of one's own ego brings its attendant dangers, Hesse was well aware, but at a time when the individual and his personal dignity had passed from sight, he considered it necessary to make an unambiguous appeal to the moral autonomy of the individual person and to point out the road that led there. Hesse did not repeat his appeals of 1918, 1919, and 1920, following the catastrophe of World War II: what he had written before still stood.

NEW BEGINNINGS IN TICINO

By the time *Demian* was published Hesse had already left his house in Berne, never to return. During the final months of 1918 his own household had collapsed completely. His wife was in a mental institution, but even when she came out any attempt to restore their marriage seemed to be out of the question. The children were boarded out with friends or in institutions. Lonely and desolate, Hesse sat in the deserted house.

> *Night rustles through the elm*
> *The garden laughs, full of ghosts.*
> *Once again I've closed my rattling window*
> *And my heart.*

Looking back on this period twenty years later, he wrote: "If I was to emerge from the horrors and losses of the war years that had so nearly destroyed me and restore meaning to my life, my only chance was through radical self-examination and change, through loosing myself from everything that had gone before and through an attempt to start afresh.

"This lasted until the spring of 1919, when I was released from the Prisoners of War Welfare Organization for which I had been working. Freedom found me alone in an empty and neglected house which had been deficient in lighting and heating for the past year. There was very little left of my former life. I therefore called it a day, packed my books and clothes and writing desk, closed up the deserted house, and began to look for some place where alone and undisturbed I could begin all over again."

His search took him to Ticino in southern Switzerland. "Good luck to the man who has possessions, is settled, faithful, and virtuous!" writes Hesse in *Wanderung* (*Excursions*), a book that resulted from that time. "I can love him, respect him, and envy him. But I have lost half my life in my attempt to emulate his virtues. I wanted to be what I was not. Of course, I wanted to be a poet, but I wanted to be a citizen as well. I wanted to be an artist and a man who used his imagination, but at the same time I wanted to possess virtue and enjoy a home. It has taken a long time to discover that one can't be and have both, that I am not a peasant but a nomad, a seeker, and a preserver. For years I have mortified myself before gods and laws— but they were no more than idols. That was my mistake, my anguish, and my complicity in the misery of the world. The way of redemption leads neither to the left nor to the right but into one's own heart, and there alone is God, and there, freedom."

In April 1919 Hesse was living in a small farmhouse just outside Minusio, near Locarno. He then stayed a few weeks in Seregno, and finally, with the help of Andreae, he found Montagnola, an hour's journey from Lugano, and at that time "a small and sleepy village set among vineyards and chestnut woods." In the village was the Casa Camuzzi, a strange palazzo-like building in the style of a baroque hunting lodge. In May 1919 he moved into the village. What started as a lonely man's sanctuary became his permanent home.

Life after the collapse now began afresh. During the summer of 1919 a new man emerged from the former wreck. Wholly reliant upon himself, he discovered a fresh urge to live awakening in him, and a new urge to create came to the fore. "My sickness seems to be over; I didn't die after all. Once again the world goes round and the sun shines for me. Once again the blue of the sky, the clouds, the sea, and the woods are reflected in my enlivened eyes; once again the world belongs to me and plays its many-voiced and magic music on my heart."

The "fullest, most exuberant, most hard-working, and most ardent" time of his life was how in retrospect he described his first year in Ticino. He was at once at work on "Klein and Wagner," and, that finished, he started and completed "Klingsor." Every day he painted and drew, met new people, and spent many an evening in the Grotto over a jug of wine. "That was Klingsor's summer. On hot days I went for walks through the villages and chestnut woods, or sat on a folding stool and tried to capture

Casa Camuzzi. Pen and ink drawing by Hesse.

something of the place's fleeting magic in water colors. On warm nights I sat up late with the doors and windows open in Klingsor's little castle, doing my best—with more success in any event than I had with the brush—to sing in words the song of this unimaginable summer. It was all this that gave birth to the painter, Klingsor.''

Klingsor, the mighty magician in Wolfram's *Parzifal,* is presented in this story as a painter. The last days of his life are a series of bewitching days full of the drunken joy of living and frenzied activity. The story opens with this stirring imagery:

"A passionate summer of swift-moving life had begun. The hot days, long as they were, flared up and away like burning streamers. The brief sultry moonlit nights were followed by brief sultry rainy nights. Swift as dreams crowded with images, the glittering weeks moved feverishly on.

"Just back home after a night walk, Klingsor stood on the narrow stone balcony of his studio. Below him, dizzyingly precipitate, the old terrace gardens dropped away, a densely shadowed tangle of treetops, palms, cedars, chestnuts, judas trees, red beech, and eucalyptus, intertwined with climbing plants, lianas, wisterias. Above the blackness of the trees the large glossy leaves of the summer magnolias gleamed pallidly, the huge snow-white blossoms half-shut among them, large as human heads, pale as moon and ivory. From the massed leafage, penetrating and rousing, a tartly sweet smell of lemons drifted toward him. From some indefinite distance languorous music winged its way to him, perhaps a guitar, perhaps a piano; there was no saying."

Klingsor suspected that death was not far off. He was aware of transience and decline. "'Each has his stars,' Klingsor said slowly. 'Each has his faith. I believe in only one thing: in doom. We are driving in a carriage on the

The painter.

edge of an abyss, and the horses have already shied. We are immersed in doom, all of us; we must die, we must be born again. The great turning point has come for us.'''
And now Klingsor began to paint his own picture, ''an enormous confession, a ruthless, crying, moving, terrifying peccavi.'' In restless, burning, ecstatic days and nights, half mad, half intoxicated, he struggled with his picture, his self-portrait, his last effort. In the story's feverish,

magnificent final chapter we read: "They say: this is man, ecce homo, here is the weary, greedy, wild, childlike, and sophisticated man of our late age, dying European man who wants to die, overstrung by every longing, sick from every vice, enraptured by knowledge of his doom, ready for any kind of progress, ripe for any kind of retrogression, submitting to fate and pain like the drug addict to his poison, lonely, hollowed-out, age-old, at once Faust and Karamazov, beast and sage, wholly exposed, wholly without ambition, wholly naked, filled with childish dread of death and filled with weary readiness to die."

But this was also the writer's own confession, an act of liberation. In a letter to Mathilde Schwarzenbach he wrote: "I have renewed my former sense of possessing a soul that in miniature represents a small segment of human development, and of the truth that basically the smallest internal whisper is as important as war and peace are to the external world . . . I am minded once again to do battle with form in order to find a suitable structure through which to express the new things I have to say."

Klingsor reminds us of the painter Van Gogh, but the story's external framework, the countryside, and so on, are in fact only a thinly veiled picture of what Hesse endured in those first months in Ticino. Hesse appears in the stories as the poet Thu Fu, Louis der Grausame has the characteristic of the painter Moilliet, Josef Englert hides behind Jupp the Magician (Englert was the noted architect in whose house Hesse had spent many a happy hour), and behind the queen of the mountains is Ruth Wenger, later to become his second wife. Hesse enjoyed burying people in his books in this fashion, particularly his closest friends. The best example of this practice is *Die Morgenlandfahrt* (*The Journey to the East*).

Hesse's encounter with the countryside in Ticino considerably enriched his descriptive language, making it more effective and colorful, an advance that could hardly have been made had he not at the same time done a great deal of painting. His first awkward efforts dated from Berne, as *Demian* shows, and were done in connection with the psychoanalysis he was then undergoing. "As I have no time for thinking or writing, I have taken to painting in my few free moments . . . but I am not competing with anyone, for I paint only imaginary things," Hesse wrote from Berne to Hans Sturzenegger on December 25, 1916. But painting now became a more serious affair, though nonetheless enjoyable for that, as day after day he set out with paint box, drawing block, and folding stool to sit by the edge of the woods or by the roadside and paint mountains, trees, and houses, and the churches and chapels of the Coilina d'Oro. It was the pleasure of it that spurred him on, not artistic ambition. Soon he had produced numerous small water colors. ". . . one day I discovered a brand new pleasure. At the late age of forty I suddenly began to paint. Not that I considered myself a painter, or even wanted to become one. But painting is a wonderful activity: it makes one happier and more patient . . ."

In *Gedichten des Malers* (*Poems of the Painter*) and also in *Excursions,* both published in 1920, the latter being one of Hesse's most charming books, we find for the first time a combination of poems, prose pieces, and pictures. They are guileless and unpretentious books. But these are the very qualities that make *Excursions* so attractive. It charmed André Gide, who spoke of its unaffected manner, and of the "complete and harmonious oneness with the outside world" that characterizes both writing and pictures. Hesse also illustrated larger manuscripts such as *Piktors Verwandlungen* (*Piktor's Metamorphoses*) and *The Difficult Path* with his own work, and by selling these decorated manuscripts he was able to keep body and soul together at times when he was receiving very little income from his books. Painting afforded him pleasure and relaxation well into old age, and he would often decorate letters and poems with elegant water-color miniatures.

"Using sepia I first draw a small lake, a few mountains, and a cloud in the sky, and then erect a small imaginary village on the side of the hill in the foreground, give the sky a little cobalt, the lake a shimmer of Prussian blue, the village some ocher or Naples yellow, everything thinly spread, and then I'm happy to see how the soft, absorbent paper tones down the colors and holds them together. With a dampened finger I rub the sky a little paler and in general get along very well with my simple little palette . . . it makes a pleasant pastime and it doesn't bother me at all that what I produce is without artistic value."

The first number of *Vivos Voco*, a monthly journal jointly edited by Hesse and Woltereck, was published in October 1919. The Preface to the first number starts: "Our monthly journal, its name taken from the old bell epigraph, is not the child of any particular program or platform but is the result rather of the several years of work the editors put in when they were the joint directors of the Prisoners of War Welfare Organization . . . Together we not only observed a considerable portion of the misery of the times, but studied it closely and did all we could to fight it.

"Our appeal to the living, particularly to the young, is the appeal for help and for co-strugglers against the dangers of our times . . . In these immediate post-war years, there is no political, economic, scientific, or artistic question more urgent than that of caring for the young and the weak."

Through this involvement in a journal whose object was to assist in the creation of a new Germany and a new way of life, and which, along with treatments of practical social questions, chiefly highlighted educational problems, Hesse demonstrated that even in convalescent seclusion he did not consider himself relieved of responsibility for the events of his times, but on the contrary wished, as a writer, to contribute to the rebuilding of Germany. Although he had little to do with the journal's political, social, or economic sections, and wrote for them only very occasionally, he took great pains to impress his personal stamp on its literary section. The journal published excerpts from *Klingsor,* the important short story "Klein und Wagner," the "Weg der Liebe" ("The Way of Love"), and "Gedanken zu Dostojewskijs Idiot" ("Comments on Dostoevski's Idiot"). His contributions contained no practical suggestions but instead invited his readers to examine themselves in depth and to champion a simple, clear, ethical attitude. ". . . the heroism that looks so fine in the orders of the day or in reports of victory from the battlefield is a mere sentimentality. When a conquered soldier takes his life at the foot of his flag, or when one who has fallen on hard times wants to hear no more of friendship, love, and goodness, because he feels that they have all let him down, we are witnessing the sort of behavior that only impresses theatergoers. There is nothing heroic about gnashing one's teeth, and to stuff one's hands in one's pockets and savor thoughts of revenge is merely deplorable."

Hesse's editorship of the journal (its net proceeds were passed on to children's welfare organizations) lasted until December 1922. But he continued to write and review books for it. In a review written in 1922 he came out unequivocally against German anti-semitism. "A little book called *Verrat am Deutschtum* [*The Betrayal of Germanness*] by Wilhelm Michel (Verlag P. Steegemann, Hanover) gives me an opportunity to say something about one of the most ugly and foolish forms of nationalism demonstrated nowadays by some young Germans. I refer to the idiotic and pathological baiting of Jews indulged in by the swastika bards and their numerous, primarily student, followers. We have had anti-semitism before and on that occasion it was silly, like all such movements, but it didn't do much harm. But the form of it with us now among misled German youth does a lot of harm, because it prevents these young people from seeing the world as it is and because disastrously it encourages the tendency to seek out a scapegoat on which to blame everything that goes wrong. Whether one loves the Jews or not, they are men, frequently much more clever, more active, and better men than their fanatical opponents. If they do wrong, then we can fight them just as we fight any other evil . . . But to make a whole race the scapegoat for the evil in the world and for the thousand serious faults of the German people is such a vile exhibition of decadence that the damage it does outweighs tenfold such damage as might ever have been done by the Jews themselves."

Writing of this sort brought Hesse a fresh outbreak of personal abuse. The journal *Oberdeutschland* branded *Vivos Voco* an international pacifists' journal, and said: "Our youth and our students care nothing for the pacifism propagated by their journal and in such a curiously agitated way by their contributor Hermann Hesse." Defamatory and slanderous letters poured into his letterbox, most of them from students. But Hesse commented: "Without these bitter and hateful reactions I would not be inclined to continue much longer with our little journal but would rather concern myself with youth and with everyday things. But how depressing is the spirit, or rather the lack of it, shown by these letters and attitudes!"

The year 1919 was a highpoint in which Hesse experienced intensely the joys of living and working. There were not enough hours in the day to see everything through. But the next year, Hesse tells us in his *Tagebuch des Jahres 1920 (Journal for 1920)*, "was quite the least productive year of my life, and therefore the saddest . . . For eighteen months I've been living almost like a snail, slowly and sparingly, the flame turned right down." The diary entries, not published until 1932, are a valuable key to an understanding of his writing and of his understanding of the poetic life between the publication of *Klingsor's Last Summer* and the appearance of *Siddhartha:* "If one regards writing as a confession of personal convictions (and limited though this might be, that is the only way in which I can visualize it), then art must be seen as a long, ever-changing, winding path whose object is to express the personality, the ego, of the artist so completely and so exhaustively that by the finish this ego is, as it were, so exposed and exhausted as to be burned out and speechless."

Understood in this sense, the function of art is to a certain extent identical with the function of private confession. But the artist is no saint: he will remain the prisoner of his own complexes no matter how sincere his confession, whereas the saint will conquer himself by surrendering himself to God. The artist's confession tends constantly towards self-justification. His confession readily becomes a selfish search for pleasure in himself. Hesse saw this danger. The imitation of Christ that inspired the saints attracted him strongly, but he knew that he was an artist and that, being rooted in "deeply religious but totally Protestant and schismatic soil," it was not a line he could pursue.

His journal entries are like moments of unresolved introspection, unanswered questions. But they are a part of the inquest Hesse held at that time into his life and work. Little of what he had achieved so far struck him as worth preserving, and very careful sifting preceded the collection of poems that appeared in 1921. He rejected most of his lyrical work. He would not publish a collected edition of his works and in his Preface for his selected works he explained: "Much of the writing that years ago I considered beautiful and successful now appeared ridiculous and worthless. And all these pieces were about me, reflected my particular path, my secret dreams, and hopes, my own bitter griefs. Even those books in which I had honestly thought while writing them to portray destinies and conflicts that were not mine, in fact sang the same song, breathed the same air, and interpreted the same destiny—mine."

Only very rarely in his first years there did Hesse go away from Montagnola. Even the area around Lugano remained unvisited. A few lectures and reading commissions that the need for cash obliged him to accept took him to St. Gallen, Zurich, and Berne. And now and again he visited the Wenger family in Delsberg. In the early summer of 1921 he spent a few weeks in Zurich, where he visited Andreae, Bucherer, Schoeck, Ilona Durigo, saw a lot of Ruth Wenger, and several times called on Jung in Kilchberg. But the rest of the time he spent in remote seclusion in the Casa Camuzzi, where an old woman from the village cooked and kept house for him. Devaluation had reduced his German royalties to a trickle that didn't suffice even for his frugal way of life. Swiss friends, particularly Georg Reinhart and Fritz Leuthold, helped him out with money. Cuno Amiet provided a home for Bruno, the eldest son. ". . . I was by now no more than a humble, burned out writer, a shabby and suspicious stranger, who lived on milk, rice, and macaroni, wore his old suits until they dropped to bits, and in the autumn came home from the woods with a supper of chestnuts. But the experiment that was at the heart of the matter was successful, and in spite of the things that made these years difficult, they were beautiful and fruitful. As though awakened from a nightmare that had gone on for years, I now broke out into freedom, air, sun, solitude, and work.''

Hugh Ball and his wife became close friends. Ball described his first meeting with Hesse in *Die Flucht aus der Zeit.* ''We have made the acquaintance of the author of *Demian.* It was midday as a slim, young-looking man entered the room. His features were sharply chiseled and one could see that he had known suffering. He glanced quickly round the walls and then looked us hard in the eyes. We offered him a chair and I lit a fire in the stove. Soon we were sitting and talking as though we had known one another for years.''

Ball, who died prematurely in 1927—but not before he had completed his last book, a biography of Hesse presented to him on the occasion of his fiftieth birthday—became one of Hesse's closest friends. ''My personal relationship to Ball, one that over the years grew from respect and admiration to deep love, had two particular supports, two properties common to us both. Different though we were in nature, ancestry, and ambitions, we had two important things in common: our religious background . . . and secondly our reaction to the war. From family and childhood we had both brought with us ancient traditions, high ideals, sensitive consciences, and an exalted concept of what it is to be human. Also we had both experienced in the war the visible collapse, the dreadful explosion, of intellectual and spiritual Europe, and this calamity struck us both in much the same way: not merely shock in the face of murder and misery but as a trumpet call to our own consciences.'' On December 16, 1927, the day Ball was buried, Hess wrote of him: ''We found in you not only a dependable, magnanimous, and forbearing friend, a dear and thoughtful colleague, a wonderful companion and opponent for hours and nights of talk, argument, and dialectical play; you were not only a gifted, agreeable, interesting, profound person whom we could love and admire and with whom we could talk in deep friendship—you were something much more than all this: you were our model."

Few visitors came to Montagnola. But T. S. Eliot made his way there to meet the author of *Glance into Chaos,* a book he greatly admired. Hesse wrote this book about Dostoevsky in 1919. He had seen in the great man's works, particularly in *The Brothers Karamazov,* a prophecy of the collapse of Europe and of the arrival in the West of a totally amoral way of thought and perception: "Half Europe, at least half Eastern Europe, is on the road to chaos, travels drunk and in dreadful delusion along the edge of the abyss, singing hymnically and as one inebriated, as Dmitri Karamazov sang. The citizen is offended by the singing, but he smiles; the saint and the seer hear it with tears in their eyes."

In the winter of 1919 Hesse started work on *Siddhartha,* a book based on his knowledge of India. After a good beginning he dried up. "It was then that I saw—not, of course, for the first time, but more clearly than ever before—that it is absurd to want to write something one has never experienced. In the long intervals in which I was unable to work on *Siddhartha,* I had to recollect and deepen my memories of the life of asceticism and meditation before I could once again find my way in the world of the Indian spirit that I had found holy and congenial since early youth."

Siddhartha was published in 1922. The first part was dedicated to Romain Rolland; the second, completed one and a half years later, to Wilhelm Gundert, who had himself dug deep into the languages, literatures, and religions of the East. The book describes the path taken by Siddhartha, the son of an aristocratic Brahmin family, who leaves home, joins a quietist sect and becomes a Samana, because the spiritual world in which he had grown up had lost its attraction. But as a penitent ascetic he fails to find the knowledge he thirsts for, just as he fails to find it in his encounter with Gotama Buddha. Govinda, his friend and companion, follows the Illustrious One. But still no mysteries are revealed. He continues on his way and steeps himself in the world of the senses. Kamala, the most beautiful of the courtesans, becomes his teacher. Success in business makes him rich and powerful. But disgusted, and in himself still a Samana, he leaves the world of meretricious display. He awakens from his despair to a new life and, as assistant to Vasudeva the ferryman, learns the mystery of the river, of permanence despite outward change, unity within eternal change: "The lament of those who yearn, the laughter of the wise, the cry of indignation, and the groan of the dying. They were all interwoven and interlocked, entwined in a thousand ways. And all the voices, all the goals, all the yearnings, all the sorrows, all the pleasures, all the good and evil, all of them together was the world. All of them together was the stream of events, the music of life. When Siddhartha listened attentively to this river, to this song of a thousand voices; when he did not listen to the sorrow or laughter, when he did not bind his soul to any one particular voice and absorb it in his Self, but heard them all, the whole, the unity; then the great song of a thousand voices consisted of one word: Om—perfection."

"Siddhartha" is Sanskrit for "he who has achieved his goal"; and the Hesse of *Siddhartha* had discovered afresh the harmony of the world. This can also be seen in the calm, measured, and musical style in which the book is written. Hesse himself said the book was the fruit of "nearly twenty years of familiarity with the thought of India and China." Whereas *Aus Indien* (*India*) (1913) was limited to surface impressions of India, *Siddhartha* shows how deeply he had immersed himself in the Eastern spiritual world. He was all the more pleased, therefore,

103

when an Indian scholar whom he met at an international congress in Lugano told him, having heard him read *Siddhartha's* final chapter, how surprised he was to come across a European capable of reaching to the heart of the Indian way of thought. *Siddhartha* was well received in India and has so far been translated into eight Indian languages.

The end of *Siddhartha* is more Taoist than Indian. For Hesse the book was only a milestone along his path of deepening interest in the Eastern world. In the coming years, the point of primary interest was to change from Indian to Chinese religions and philosophies.

Once again, if on this occasion in somewhat exotic dress, Hesse used his character's life story as a means of telling his own. One can discern in *Siddhartha* an attempt to liberate himself from his father's pietism; and the author himself confirmed that *Siddhartha* was a representation of his own outlook: "That Siddhartha places love above knowledge, that he rejects dogma and accords pride of place to the experience of unity, might be taken as a bow towards Christianity, indeed as a genuinely Protestant characteristic."

THE STEPPENWOLF

Hesse's marriage was dissolved in the summer of 1923, and in the same year he was granted Swiss citizenship. "When I saw during the post-war years how with one accord Germany was sabotaging the Republic, and that it had learned nothing from its previous mistakes, it became an easy matter for me to assume Swiss nationality, something I would not have been able to do during the war, in

1927.

spite of my condemnation by the German *Machtpolitik*,"
he explained in 1945 in a letter to Bishop Wurm of
Württemberg.

From 1923 onwards, Hesse spent the winter months and
sometimes the spring in Switzerland. He spent two win-
ters in Basle, and in the late autumn of 1923 he visited
Stuttgart and Freiburg to give some readings, this being
his first visit to Germany for some considerable time. In
January 1924 he married Ruth Wenger, daughter of the
Swiss writer Lisa Wenger. ". . . I neither want marriage
particularly nor am I well suited to it, but in this connec-

tion life and destiny are more powerful than my thoughts and wishes," he had said in a letter six months earlier. But his second marriage didn't last long. It was officially dissolved in the spring of 1927.

From 1925 to 1931 Hesse spent every winter in Zurich in a small apartment in the Schanzengraben, lent to him by his friends Alice and Fritz Leuthold whom he had met during his Indian journey. For many years Fritz Leuthold had been a businessman in Siam and had assembled a large collection of Asian art that now decorated his beautiful Zurich house, giving it a touch of the East that Hesse found very congenial. The summer months Hesse often spent with the Weltis near Berne. Friedrich Emil Welti was an able aristocratic historian, and he and his second wife became close friends of Hesse. Later Hesse dedicated his poem "Orgelspiel" ("Organ Music") to Welti, and the poem "Sommertag auf einem alten Landsitz" ("A Summer Day at an Old Country House") is an evocation of "Lohn," their country house. Other close friends were Georg Reinhart, the art collector and patron from Winterthur, Max Wassmer and his wife, and Elsy and Hans C. Bodmer from Zurich.

In 1923, on account of serious rheumatism and following medical advice, Hesse started his annual visits to Baden, the health resort. Not liking the swarms of summer visitors, he would go there in late autumn, spending most of his time in his hotel, the Verena-Hof, punctiliously carrying out his doctor's orders. In *Aufzeichnung bei einer Kur in Baden* (*Notes during a Health Cure in Baden*), which he wrote later, he recorded his impressions of hotel life in Baden. "In two and a half decades I have experienced much in this house, thought and dreamed of many things, written much. At one time or another, the manuscripts of *Narcissus and Goldmund, The Journey to the East,* and *The Glass Bead Game* all found their way into the

106

drawer of my writing desk there; and hundreds of letters, journal entries, and a few dozen poems were written in its rooms; colleagues and friends from many countries and from many periods of my life visited me there. I recall many happy and convivial drinking evenings but also many miserable days, times of frenzied work, of tiredness and sterility. There was hardly a corner of the house, or for that matter of the town either, that lacked associations, often so many that they were there in layers, one above the other . . . On the third floor was that cheerful, three-windowed room in which I wrote the two poems "Nacht-gedanken" ("Night Thoughts") and "Gesinnung" ("At-titudes"), the former in the night after I had read in the papers the first reports of the Jewish pogroms and of the burning of the synagogues. And in the house's other wing, a few months before my fiftieth birthday, I wrote *Gedichte im Krankenbett* (*Poems from My Sickbed*). And it was down-stairs in the hall that I had the first news of the disap-pearance of my brother Hans, and in the same place a day later heard of his death."

During his first year in Baden, Hesse wrote the *Psycho-logia Balnearia oder Glossen eines Badener Kurgastes* (*Notes of a Baden Patient*), a book that in later editions was called *Kurgast, Aufzeichnungen einer Badener Kur* (*Patient, Notes of a Boden Cure*). It was dedicated to Franz Xaver Mark-walder, the proprietor of the hotel, and his brother, Dr. Josef Markwalder. A note in the first, privately printed, edition reads: "The *Psychologia Balnearia* was conceived in the course of two visits to the Baden health resort, spring and autumn 1923, and written partly in Baden and partly in Montagnola."

Later Hesse commented: "Inspired partially by the unaccustomed leisure of health resort and hotel life, and partially by a few fresh acquaintanceships with people and books, I experienced in those summer months a mood of introspection and self-examination midway between *Siddhartha* and *Steppenwolf,* a mood in which I could play the spectator both of myself and of my immediate environment, an ironic and playful desire to inspect and analyze the fleeting moment, a period of suspense between sluggish indolence and intensive work.'' He also maintained that he had always considered *Notes of a Baden Patient* to be one of his better books. It is not concerned with Baden, its countryside, or its people, but exclusively with the psyche of the patient, and ultimately once again with his whole personal attitude towards the world of normal people. He described this book and its successor, *Journey to Nuremberg,* as ''attempts at honesty and humor''; and in a letter dated January 19, 1924, he wrote: ''Beneath a half-jocular façade you will find in my book the most personal and earnest of my confessions.''

In the eyes of Hesse the poet, Hesse as visitor to the health resort lives in contradiction with himself and his environment. Like the poet, he suffers from the antinomies of life, from the tension between its two poles. ''I should like to express this duality. I should like to write chapters and sentences in which melody and countermelody are clearly and simultaneously apparent, in which variety is set off against unity and what is humorous against what is serious. For that is where my life is, in the alternation between two poles, in the fluctuations between the world's two chief pillars. I want to point out constantly and with infectious enthusiasm how blissfully varied the world is, and with equal constancy remind people that this variety is based on an underlying unity.'' And elsewhere: ''My destiny is that I, a poet, must try again and again to subdue the world by thought instead of art.'' This was the problem that was at the heart of his discussions with Jung in summer 1921.

The chapter called ''The Dutchman'' is rather like a

therapeutic study. Herr vom Haag's heedless, harmless but perpetually audible statements about life that Hesse can hear through the wall of his room drive him, in his irritable and over-excited condition, to distraction. Hesse storms into his neighbor's room to have it out with him. It is then shown how through self-observation, empathy, and finally a type of mystical union with his opponent, he succeeds in conquering hate and changing it into love.

Hesse concerned himself constantly with the question of how a man, particularly the artist, who faces the normal healthy man much as one who is sick does, can happily acclimatize himself in the world of reality, of how he can free himself from its relativity. But only in this short complex book, this attempt ''to exhibit a tiny piece of life with maximum truthfulness and honesty,'' did he manage it with such mastery, self-irony, and humor.

Temporally and autobiographically, *Notes of a Baden Patient* is related to *Journey to Nuremberg,* a book that tells of a reading tour in southern Germany and that, like *Notes of a Baden Patient,* mixes humor and irony with fundamental statements. In the late autumn of 1925, Hesse was invited to read from his own books in several south German towns, and after some initial hesitation he decided to accept. ''In public readings I experience not only the recluse's reservations about public occasions—these are not difficult to conquer—but I also come up against some fundamental and deeply anchored disorders and tensions. To put the matter much too briefly and crudely, these pertain to my distrust of literature generally. They attack me not only during these readings but much more strongly while I'm working. I set no store by contemporary literature. I appreciate of course that every period must have its own literature, just as it will have its own politics, ideals, and fashions. But I cannot rid myself of the conviction that contemporary writing is something insubstantial and sorry, a seed grown on poor soil, doubtless interesting and full of problems worthy of pursuit, but hardly something that can mature or that is capable of producing long-term results. Consequently, I can only consider the work of contemporary German writers (my own included) to be in some way inadequate and derivative; I detect everywhere a suspicion of routine, lifeless models of what things should be. On the other hand, a transitional literature, writing that has become problematical and uncertain, can perform the useful function of confessing with maximum honesty its own poverty and the poverty of its times. There are, therefore, many fine and well-structured books by contemporary writers that I can no longer enjoy or welcome, whereas I can feel sympathy for several crudely written books by our youngest writers because of their attempt at unreserved sincerity . . . This is the tension that goes right through my own little world and my writing . . .''

Traveling via Locarno. Zurich, and Tuttlingen, Hesse first visited his friend Wilhelm Häcker in Blaubeuren. He gave a reading in Ulm, visited friends, inspected the barracks, the stations, and the cathedral, and wondered if he had not after all merely neglected, rather than found it impossible, to adapt himself to "reality as it actually is."
''And once again I felt that tension between the two opposed poles, felt the swaying of the insubstantial bridge across the gap between reality and ideal, between reality and beauty. And the bridge was humor. Yes, with humor it was all tolerable, even the railway stations, even the barracks, and even the public readings.''

This journey led him onward to Augsburg, Munich, and finally to Nuremberg. "I saw St. Lorenz and St. Sebald, saw the Rathans with its courtyard where the fountain stands with such ineffable grace. I saw all this and it was all very beautiful, but also it was all surrounded by a large,

110

loveless, dreary industrial town, full of rattling machines and noisy automobiles. Everything trembled gently under the tempo of another age that builds no vaulted ceilings and sees no place for fountains as gentle as flowers in peaceful courtyards. Everything was ripe for collapse within the next hour, for it had lost its purpose and its soul."

The journey, and with it the book, which is rather like a sentimental intermezzo between books of a quite different type, ended with a visit to Thomas Mann in Munich, a meeting with Joachim Ringelnatz, and a visit to the theater.

"It may be important to great thinkers to examine the world, to explain and despise it. But I think it is only important to love the world, not to despise it, not for us to hate each other, but to be able to regard the world and ourselves and all beings with love, admiration and respect," wrote Hesse towards the end of *Siddhartha*. But for Hesse the goal that Siddhartha achieved could be no more than a step along the way. After only a few years, whose outer but not interior content was documented in *Notes of a Baden Patient* and *Journey to Nuremberg*, Hesse surprised and terrified his readers with *Steppenwolf*, a book that relentlessly documented the Day of Judgment. In his Epilogue to *Krisis* (*Crisis*), a fragment from his journal with a few poems added, Hesse wrote: "My life is characterized by alternating periods of intense sublimation, asceticism of the spirit, and surrender to naïve sensuality, childlike behavior, foolishness, and also madness and peril. These are variations common to all men. The greater part of the darker, perhaps deeper, aspect of my life has been unconsciously concealed or palliated in my earlier poems. This, I feel, was not because I was

111

naïvely trying to destroy what was sensual in me but because I believed myself to be incapable of handling it adequately. I was a better judge of the spiritual, in the widest sense, than of the sensual . . .''

The search for truth drove Hesse to a renewed analysis of himself and of his times. His own existence, his activity, and his environment, had become hateful to him. ''Don't write me any more letters. At the moment, I find any mention of your normal, bourgeois, satisfied existence intolerable,'' he wrote in a letter at this time. It was not only the satiated, self-satisfied, bourgeois world that Hesse found intolerable, but above all the technological world and a civilization that saw itself as its own end, and that in his sensitive eyes was endangering the spirit and soul of mankind. ''The thought of the abyss gaping beneath our feet, and the feeling of being threatened by catastrophes and wars'' left him no peace.

In this mood he wrote the story of Harry Haller, the Steppenwolf, which can also be seen as a cathartic release of many of the statements Hesse wanted to make about himself. Haller's crisis, as he rises in revolt against the world that had been carrying him so far, can be seen as analogous to the pathological crisis of a man who has reached the age of fifty. But the diagnosis reveals the neurosis of a whole generation, the sickness of the age to which Haller belongs. Through Steppenwolf, the solitary animal that nothing can stop, Haller tries to resolve the tension within himself and that between himself and the world. But his life is split many ways, ''not just between two poles, instinct and spirit, or the saint and the libertine, but swings between thousands, countless, pairs of poles.'' Complete disintegration threatens, and Haller searches desperately for the center, sifting through the wreckage of his life for its elusive meaning. But he will only recover lost unity when he succeeds in penetrating the subconscious of the "magical self," if he is prepared to surrender to the chaos in his own soul, to struggle through to full self-awareness. Haller's records are therefore much more than the fantasies of a dejected idealist. They are "not an attempt to disguise or to palliate this widespread sickness of our times. They are an attempt to present the sickness itself in its actual manifestation. They mean, literally, a journey through hell, a sometimes fearful, sometimes courageous journey through the chaos of a world whose souls dwell in darkness, a journey undertaken with the determination to go through hell from one end to the other, to do battle with chaos, and to bear the evil to the full."

The book centers on this self-encounter, the journey inwards through hell. The self-encounter takes place in a strange twilight zone between dream, vision, and reality, a structural device that lends the encounter a particular intensity. Haller traverses dark labyrinths of emotion, depravity, and error, and of nihilism and cynical disgust that drive him almost to suicide. His own past is reflected in a box of many-faceted mirrors and Haller learns that that other reality that he longs for is to be found in his own inner being. "I can give you nothing that has not already its being within yourself. I can throw open to you no picture gallery but your own soul. All I can give you is the opportunity, the impulse, the key. I help you to make your own world visible. That is all."

Steppenwolf proves to be no all-resolving final solution. Haller fails the tests he is set but does not end in despair. He intends to begin the game again, to live again, and this time he would learn to laugh, as instructed: "It is time to come to your senses. You are to live and to learn to laugh. You are to learn to listen to life's radio music and to reverence the spirit behind it." Haller learns that nothing is settled by maintaining that technology, war, money-lust,

113

nationalism, and all the other hated phenomena are inferior. Instead, he finds that magnificent, timeless, and inviolable concepts lie concealed behind appearances. Transcending all that is instinctive and chaotic is a "second, superior, enduring world," the world of "immortal things, a positive, serene, suprapersonal, supratemporal world of faith." That is the point of the magic theater, for Hesse "image and mask" for what he valued most. The magic theater becomes the supra-real stage from which the divine and the spiritual can speak to man untouched by the distortions of barbaric civilization.

A golden thread shines through the confusion. It leads to Mozart. His name is among those of the immortals, and a magic power attaches to it. The book ends with the words "Mozart is waiting for me." And it is interesting to note that as early as the *Journal for 1920* Hesse had written: "At the start of this day, of this page from the colorful leaves of my life, I should like to write a particular word, a word such as 'world,' or 'sun,' a word full of magic and radiant power, full of sound and richness, fuller than full, richer than rich, a word signifying total fulfillment, total knowledge.

"And now in a flash the very word occurs to me, the magic sign for this day. I shall write it large at the top of the page: MOZART. That means: the world has meaning and we can sense this meaning allegorically through music."

Steppenwolf was published in 1927. In the spring of the same year, after recovering from serious physical exhaustion, Hesse started work on *Narcissus and Goldmund,* a work of quite a different type and his only book to present a resolution of the tensions between spirit and eros. In the course of his work on this book he wrote a short piece called "Eine Arbeitsnacht" ("A Night's Work") in which he says: "I am now at work on something new and a character is emerging who for a while will serve as symbol and bearer of my life experience, thoughts, and problems. The emergence of these mythical figures (Peter Camenzind, Knulp, Demian, Siddhartha, Harry Haller, and so on) is the creative center from which everything else flows. Almost every book I have written has been a spiritual biography. Central to each are not stories, entanglements, and tensions, but monologues in which a particular person's (in other words, the mythical figure's) relationship to the world and to himself is put under the microscope."

Like the earlier books, *Narcissus and Goldmund* is a spiritual biography. But, since in this particular book the antitheses of logos and eros, the paternal and the maternal principles, are embodied in the two different forms of a complementary friendship, the tension does not end in dissonance, but resolves itself in genuine polarity. The story is set in the Middle Ages. Narcissus, the scholarly young monk, develops a passionate friendship for Goldmund, but whereas Narcissus is an ascetic, bent on the pursuit of the life of the spirit through monasticism, Goldmund travels out into the world. He is a man of the flesh, and seeks life and women.

Erotic love hardly occurs at all in Hesse's other books but it is poetically expressed here. Goldmund becomes a sculptor and his finest achievement, a statue of St. John the Apostle, bears the features of Narcissus. He finds it impossible to remain long in one place and in the course of his wanderings undergoes several adventures. He is always striking into fresh territory, lusting for new women. Finally he returns to the monastery of Mariabronn, where he dies in the arms of his friend. The story is a parable in which the old contrast between the artist and the thinker, between the creative representation of the world and the intellectual's reflective penetration of it, is resolved into

115

On a ski trip with Ninon Dolbin, née Ausländer.

harmony and higher unity. Both characters fulfill themselves: Goldmund in experiencing and tasting the world of
the flesh, and Narcissus through his strict adherence to the
spirit.

The book enjoyed a considerable and lasting success.
Many readers and critics, relieved to have *Steppenwolf*
behind them, praised the story as Hesse's most beautiful
and poetic achievement, and as the happiest expression of
his story-telling skill. Hesse himself reacted with slight
mockery to the book's warm welcome, and in a letter to
Erwin Ackerknecht observed: ''*Goldmund* delights people,
but it is in no way better than *Steppenwolf*, where the theme

is expressed more clearly and which has the structural composition of a sonata. But our good old German readers can tackle *Goldmund* with a pipe between their teeth, dream about the Middle Ages, and imagine life to be as beautiful and melancholy as they like, without any need to consider their own lives, occupations, wars, civilization, or any such thing. Once more they have a book after their own tastes. But none of that matters much; in the end it boils down to that small handful of people . . ."

Hesse's fiftieth birthday, summer 1927, was not celebrated with all the pomp and circumstance that attended Thomas Mann's. He did not like public acclamation. But among the small number of Swiss friends who celebrated it with him was the Austrian art historian Ninon Dolbin, née Ausländer. Though they had corresponded for several years they had not met until the previous year, and then only by chance. From 1927 onwards they lived together. She remained until his death the understanding partner that he so badly needed.

Hesse lived in the Casa Camuzzi until 1931. He was one of the few of the strange Palazzo's many previous tenants to stay so long. "In this house I enjoyed and suffered from the most intense loneliness, gained comfort from writing and painting much, and became more fondly familiar with the place than with any other since childhood. In my painting and my writing I have frequently expressed the gratitude I owe this house." But now that he had somebody else to think about as well as himself, he had to find a larger and more comfortable house: "At this point a dream came true. One spring evening in 1930 we were sitting and talking in the 'Arch' in Zurich. The conversation turned to houses and building and there was mention of the comments I had occasionally made in this connection. My friend B. laughed suddenly and said to me: 'You shall have the house!'" It was Dr. H. C. Bodmer, a helpful friend of many year's standing. He built a house according to Hesse's own basic design and presented it to him for his lifetime. The "Casa Hesse" was built above and slightly removed from the village of Montagnola, hidden behind trees and shrubbery. It had a magnificent view across the Lake of Lugano to its Italian shore, and also of San Salvatore and the peaks of Monte Generoso.

MONTAGNOLA

In an essay entitled "Tessiner Herbsttag" ("An Autumn Day in Ticino"), Hesse described how for twelve years he lived through Ticino's late summer and autumn and enviously watched the farmers and winegrowers at work. "To be fully at home somewhere, to love a particular piece of land, and to build on it rather than merely observe and paint it, to participate in the unassuming joy of the farmers and shepherds, in the exuberance of the pastoral scene, in the two-thousand-year-old rhythm of the rural calendar, struck me as a fine and enviable lot, even though, having once tried it myself, I had discovered it was not enough to bring happiness. But once more the opportunity had arisen, had fallen into my lap like a ripe chestnut falls from the tree onto the hat of a passer by: one had only to open the fruit and eat it. Contrary to all expectations, I was once again a settled man and held a piece of land if not as my own at least as a lifelong tenant. No sooner was our house built and we in proud possession

Casa Hesse, Montagnola.

of it than another stretch of peasant life began, so familiar
to me from previous memories . . ."

The garden dropped steeply southwards away from the
house and, as once before in Gaienhofen, work in it
became part of the natural rhythm of the day. Shrubs,
trees, and flowers were planted, and up on the slope
where the wood gave way to the meadow a small bamboo
plantation was established. A few years later it was a thick
and vigorous growth through which a narrow path ran
beneath the vaulted stems. "The experience of being
settled, of possessing a home, the feeling of kinship with
flowers, trees, earth, source, the feeling of responsibility
for a small piece of land, for fifty trees, for a few flower
beds, for fig and peach trees," became a necessary and
happy complement to the work of a writer who had always
disliked town life. The serenity of Hesse's major later
books, those he wrote in the last thirty years of his life, is
rooted in the happy balance between his life as a writer
and his practical involvement in the rhythm of nature.

The house, with its large windows and its terraces,

looked onto the garden and the valley below. On the first floor there was an inner sanctum called "the studio" to which Hesse could retire when he did not feel inclined to work in his study proper on the ground floor. The latter, its writing desk covered with papers, pictures, books, manuscripts, and painting gear, also served as reference library and mail room. Next door was the combined music room and main library, where guests were received. This room also had a view across the valley. Hesse's library contained several thousand books ordered according to national literatures. The largest sections in the library were those concerned with philosophy, psychology,. and history. One of Hesse's shorter writings is called *Eine Bibliothek der Weltliteratur* (*A Library of World Literature*) and that is what this room was; in no way an arbitrary collection of books, but rather a carefully chosen selection of great personal importance to Hesse, who had amassed them over many years of constant reading.

Hesse wrote many short pieces with such titles as "On Reading," "Living with Books," "The Lure of the Book," and he regarded it as one of his duties to communicate enthusiasm for books and reading, and to introduce people to the works of the great writers.

Hesse saw the study of world literature as an indispensable way of "giving life meaning, interpreting the past, and preparing oneself to meet the future without fear." In *A Library of World Literature* Hesse explained that study such as this means "familiarizing oneself gradually with the massive treasury of thoughts, experiences, symbols, fantasies, and utopian dreams that the past has bequeathed to us in the works of writers and thinkers of many nations. It is an endless journey . . . its goal is not merely to read and know as much as possible but to acquire some inkling of the breadth and richness of what man has conceived and striven for by studying a personal selection of his greatest

120

The view from the garden, Montagnola.

books.'' But the true reader will approach his study with love: ''Reading without love, knowledge without respect, formation without deep personal involvement, are some of the most deadly sins against the spirit.'' The description that followed of an ''ideal'' small library of world literature, itself significant in regard to Hesse's own relationship to literature, offers a striking survey of national literatures, and witnesses to the breadth of his own interests.

Just as he had done earlier in Gaienhofen and then again in the course of his work for the Prisoners of War Welfare Organization, Hesse did much during the fifteen years immediately after the First World War to prepare new editions of literature that he considered important. There is not space in this monograph to mention even the titles of all the books he edited, inspired, or furnished with forewords or epilogues. But mention should at least be made of two series: *Merkwürdige Geschichten* and *Merkwürdige Geschichten und Menschen* (*Unusual Stories and People*). These were collections of anecdotes from the lives of Hölderlin, Novalis, the Brentanos (brother and sister),

121

and Schubart, together with stories and legends from Japan, Italy, and France. Jean Paul remained a particular favorite with Hesse. As early as 1913 he had published an abbreviated edition of *Titan; Siebenkäs,* stories and anthologies followed in later years. "In Jean Paul that mysterious Germany that though still living has for many years now been obscured by another, different, soulless Germany, gave birth to one of its most characteristic and complex spirits, one of the greatest writers of all time, whose books offer us a limitless fund of poetry."

Also worth mentioning are the *Geschichten des Mittelalters (Stories from the Middle Ages),* for which Hesse himself translated Casarius von Heisterbach's *Dialogus miraculorum;* editions of Justinius Kerner and Salomon Gessner and, by no means least, a painstakingly selected group of thirty poems by Goethe, published in 1932 to mark his centenary.

A large anthology "of the most significant and beautiful testimonies to the spirit that inspired the Romantics (1800-1850), most of which are unavailable in new editions," that Hesse prepared with Carlo, the son of his step-brother Karl Isenberg, was never published. It was organized in three volumes and was to have been called *Spirit of the Romantics.* The manuscript, now lost and presumed burned during the Second World War, was kept for years by S. Fischer Verlag, since they were uncertain about its prospects. In May 1931 Hesse offered it to another publisher, to whom he wrote: "Without exaggerating, I might be permitted to say that, a small number of philologists apart, there are few people more competent than I in the field of Romantic literature. I began to study it at the age of eighteen, and along with the literatures of India and China it has greatly influenced my own thought and writing . . . over the years we have revised the anthology several times. Everything has been taken into account, including some little known sources, and in consequence it presents the range of German Romantic writing comprehensively but concisely . . . This anthology is the largest and most important book of its type and is one that I have wanted and worked on since I was a young man."

In his work as an anthologist, Hesse drew much encouragement from the similar efforts of Hugo von Hofmannsthal. He had written respectful and enthusiastic reviews of Hofmannsthal's *Deutsche Lesebuch* and his *Deutsche Erzähler,* and, in a letter dated September 15, 1924, Hofmannsthal wrote to him: ". . . it gave me great pleasure to see that you, as one of the very few serious and conscientious writers we have, considered it worth the trouble to refer to the book [*Deutsche Erzähler*]. What you said meant a lot to me precisely because it was you who said it. I was particularly pleased about your final point: you saw that I was not only concerned to present examples of beautiful language but to make the country aware of what is possesses. I believe we must be tireless in our efforts to restore inner unity to this broken nation, not through some program or other, but by producing a type of spiritual center."

Hesse's activity as anthologist and editor also earned Thomas Mann's praise. "It is a service, a homage, a process of selecting, revising, re-presenting, and expert introducing that would be enough to occupy the whole lifetime of many a learned scholar. Here is an abundance of love (and of work!), an active pursuit of a labor of love in addition to his own deeply personal output that treats of the problem of man in his world with a complexity and richness that no other writer can equal."

Hesse's editorial activity was closely related to his activity as a book reviewer. Leafing through the card system in which between 1920 and 1936 Hesse recorded the titles of the books he had reviewed, and assuming that it is more or less complete, it can be seen that in this period he must have reviewed around a thousand books for over twenty different papers and journals. Most of the reviews and most of his essays on current literature appeared in *Neue Rundschau, Propyläen, Schwabenspiegel, Neue Zürcher Zeitung, Berliner Tageblatt,* and the *Frankfurter Zeitung.* Hesse saw his function as a reviewer in the singling out for attention of books that "in some sense or another possess something exemplary and genuine, that I can regard as fruits of our times, and which I can believe will still be worth reading tomorrow and afterwards." He once said to Jung, "I am neither analyst nor critic; if you look at the piece I sent you, you will see that only very seldom and then only in passing do I make critical comments, and I never warn readers off a book. When I come across a book I don't like, I lay it aside without writing anything about it all."

When the National Socialist Party came to power in Germany, Hesse sought out "books that others dare not review: books by Jews or Catholics, or by writers who put forward a point of view at variance with the official line." In the end, only the *Neue Rundschau* was prepared to employ him. Gradually the personal attacks on him increased—in Germany because he recommended books by Jews, and in the German emigré press in Switzerland, because he recommended books published in Germany. Under such pressures, Hesse temporarily gave up book reviewing altogether.

Among the more interesting of his essays on contemporary German literature are those he wrote in six installments, serial fashion (1935-6) for *Bonniers Literära Magasin,* Sweden's leading critical journal. Published only in Swedish, they remained almost unknown in Germany. "I believe and hope," he wrote in his introductory note, "that in the course of our investigation we shall see that buried among the squabbles and slogans there is a German literature worthy of our interest and love." Quality, not the author's standing in Germany, was Hesse's sole

At work in the vineyard.

criterion, and in consequence these essays must be included among the few comparable documents written at that time that reflected a wholly independent viewpoint. But of Hesse's own spiritual and political attitudes there could be no doubt. He was full of praise for Musil and Kafka. Long before Kafka was a well-known writer,

125

Hesse, who admired him greatly, had frequently mentioned his books, and he was particularly pleased to learn from Max Brod that Kafka had read his books with enthusiasm. Time has borne out Hesse's judgments. Nearly all the books, and there are many of them, that Hesse praised in these articles have stood the test of time, though many of them remained unknown to most German readers until after 1945.

Though Hesse started to review books again after the Second World War, he never again did as much as he had done before. But he always remained an alert and critical reader and observer of contemporary literature, and now and again in one article or another, as well as in letters to friends, he would advert to this or that discovery: Anna Seghers, Monique Saint-Helier, the lyrical writings of Oskar Loerke or the prose writings of Peter Suhrkamp; Richard Wilhelms, or Wilhelm Gundert's translation of *Bi Yen Lu.*

Hesse's knowledge of contemporary literature depended on reading rather than personal contact. He never pursued literary acquaintanceships for their own sake and was not particularly concerned to follow up in correspondence the chance encounters that sometimes occurred. Particularly in the last half of his life, when he seldom traveled and was no longer involved in the editing of journals, he chose to avoid the sort of literary life that characterizes the activities of the PEN Club and other writers' associations. On November 10, 1930, he resigned from the Prussian Academy of Writers, which had elected him a member in 1926. Even so, Hesse met many writers and several sought him out in Montagnola. The power politics of National Socialism turned the Casa Hesse into a temporary resting place for many a fugitive from oppression.

"The beds are made and tomorrow I'm expecting my first visitor from Germany," wrote Hesse at the beginning of March 1933; and a few days later: "for the last few days our guest room has been occupied by a fugitive from Germany, a socialist writer I've known for years." This was Heinrich Wiegand, who died in Italy shortly afterwards. Hesse had many visitors, and Max Hermann-Neisse must have been speaking for most of them when he wrote: "I was deeply moved and cheered once again to step outside the chaos of the times and all its madnesses into an atmosphere that had remained pure and spiritual and in which I could talk to a real writer about things that matter." Thomas Mann was also a visitor. Hesse had first met Mann in Munich before the First World War at a party given by their publisher, Samuel Fischer. They were to meet next in Nuremberg, and for a third time near St. Moritz during a winter skiing holiday. Mann wrote later: "I came to know him really well fourteen years ago when I stayed with him in Montagnola while still suffering from the shock of having just lost my own home. How I envied him then! Not only because he was hidden away there in the countryside, but mostly because he was so much farther ahead of me as regards spiritual freedom, and also because of his philosophical independence from German politics. There was nothing in those confused days more agreeable or salutary than talking with Hesse."

In his Thomas van der Trave, the glass bead game champion, Hesse presented a fine portrait of Thomas Mann, and when writing to him in June 1950 on the occasion of Mann's seventy-fifth birthday, he said: "Many things must have happened since our first pleasant Munich meeting, things that we could never have foreseen at the time, to have led to such a friendship as we now enjoy— one of the happiest and most relaxed of my later life; and behind us both there lies the difficult and often grim path that we have traveled, starting from the apparent security of our nationality, into the isolation and ostracization that followed, and from there to the fresher and a little cooler air of world citizenship which, however, has meant something quite different for you than it has for me, but which, nevertheless, has bound us together more firmly than whatever we might have had in common in those early days of moral and political innocence.''

Another visitor in the autumn of 1934 whose writings he greatly admired was Martin Buber (who had also visited Hesse in Montagnola ten years earlier). ''[The] . . . teacher and leader of the Jewish intellectual élite. As translator of the Bible, as the man responsible for rendering into German and so introducing us to Hassidic wisdom, as scholar, as writer, and finally as guide, teacher, and representative of a noble ethic and humanity, he is in the opinion of those familiar with his works one of the leading and greatest personalities in contemporary world literature,'' Hesse declared in an address to the Swedish Academy in 1949 when recommending Buber for the Nobel Prize. But much earlier, in a letter dated September 1933, he had written: ''Simply to know that a man like Martin Buber exists is a comfort and a pleasure.'' In a speech he gave on the occasion of Hesse's eightieth birthday, Buber said: ''You are congratulated today not just by those who travel eastwards [a reference to Hesse's book *Journey to the East*] and the glass bead game players [a reference to *The Glass Bead Game*]: servants of the spirit throughout the world greet you affectionately. Wherever men serve the spirit, you are loved.''

In 1935 Christoph Schrempf paid Hesse a surprise visit. Schrempf was the Swabian theologian, philosopher, Kierkegaard translator, writer, and orator who had earlier left the Church and, like Hesse, had become something of a lone wolf: "We met for the one and only time in 1935 . . . He was staying with some friends in our village and came to see me for a few hours every day. He was a small, immensely vigorous, and high-spirited old man who was as little disturbed by hour-long walks as by hour-long arguments. We became friends, and the memory of this Swabian Socrates has belonged ever since to the picture gallery of my life."

Hesse had foreseen the political turmoil Germany was now undergoing. Of this there is evidence enough in his writings and letters. In 1932, for instance, we find the following: "The barefaced denial of any blame for the war, the shifting of responsibility for Germany's troubles onto the 'enemies' and Versailles, is now breeding, in my view, a type of political stupidity, mendacity, and immaturity that will contribute very considerably to the development of another war."

Officially, Hesse was left undisturbed when the Nazis assumed power. "In the appeals to German youth to show some interest in their German writers, I find myself neither among those who are recommended nor among the *Asphaltliteraten* they are warned to beware of."

It was nevertheless maintained by some that Hesse did not come out with sufficient clarity on the side of the opposition. He refused to speak out in public against the fascist regime. "My intense emotional involvement in the war of 1914-18 all but destroyed me, and in consequence I am now unshaken in my conviction that for myself I must reject any attempt to change the world by force. And neither could I support such an attempt, not even a socialist one, nor one that was apparently desirable and just. It is always the wrong people that get killed, and even if it were the right people I do not believe in the curative and expiatory properties of killing people; and though I can see the beginnings of a decision resulting from the

129

possible culmination of party struggles in civil strife—the moral tension of the Either/Or—I shall continue to reject violence . . ."

> *Better to be killed by the fascists*
> *Than to be a fascist oneself*
> *Better to be killed by the communists*
> *Than to be a communist oneself!*

This was the beginning of the rough draft of a poem Hesse outlined during a restless night in March 1933. He never completed it. But in the same year, Hesse wrote a poem called "Besinnung" ("Reflections") into which he built his personal statement. As he told Steiner, its conclusion contained his attitude towards the prevailing political madness and was perhaps of some value as a warning:

> *Therefore even in strife*
> *We erring brothers can still love;*
> *Not judgment and hate*
> *But patient love and*
> *Loving patience lead us to*
> *Our sacred goal.*

Hesse refused to make any concessions and rejected outright the suggestion that he should prepare a fresh edition of *A Library of World Literature* with appropriate changes: "I cannot consider a book or an author inferior simply because they are so according to contemporary tastes, and I cannot delete things from my essay that are acceptable and important to me simply because a combination of exterior circumstances would have me do so."

He observed developments in Germany with horror and "deepest disgust." Fugitives increased in number, and what they had to say became increasingly depressing:

". . . only very seldom in the course of this year have I been able to get down to any real work. Perhaps being a part of the misery of our times is more important than productive activity," he wrote in a letter to Max Hermann-Neisse.

The Third Reich neither burned nor banned Hesse's books. Careful examination shows that between 1933 and 1945 twenty books were published with a print number totaling 481,000, though of this figure 250,000 are accounted for by a new edition of the story *In the ' 'Old Sun,''*

With his wife, Ninon.

and 70,000 by *Vom Baum des Lebens* (*The Tree of Life*), a selection of poetry. During the same period, ten titles were published in Switzerland, totaling 35,000 copies. Clearly, then, a very large readership kept faith with Hesse.

But official Germany was suspicious of him. A widely sold encyclopedia of literature (suitably edited after 1945) described him as "a lonely, sensitive, aesthetic, and eccentric poet" who "was remote from the development of the people's Germany." In reports of his sixtieth birthday the press made out that "inner solitariness separates him from the growing powers of the emergent German community."

He was sharply attacked in *Neue Literatur,* a journal edited by Will Vesper, on account of the articles he had written for *Bonniers Literära Magasin*. The writer was indignant about Hesse's laudatory mentions of Mann, Kafka, Polgar, Ernst Bloch, Gertrud von le Fort, and Stefan Zweig, and even more about a sentence such as: "Most of contemporary Germany's *belles lettres* bears the stamp of transience and is not to be taken seriously." Under the heading "In Our Opinion," it was said that Hesse "is betraying contemporary German writing to Germany's enemies and to the Jews. This shows what depths a man can sink to who has become accustomed to sitting at table with Jews and eating their bread. The German writer Hermann Hesse has taken over the role of betrayer of the people formerly held by Jews. Supporting Jews and culture Bolsheviks, he helps to spread false and damaging impressions of his fatherland." In a later issue of the same journal it was said: "It needs to be declared publicly that Hesse is a perfect example of how the Jews can poison the German soul"; and again: "he has deserted his people in their hour of need so as to take refuge behind his Swiss nationality."

But alongside this sort of abuse over voices were heard

in his defense. An issue of the *Neue Rundschau* published to mark Hesse's sixtieth birthday contained not only the first publication of his *Indischer Lebenslauf* (*Indian Living*) but also a letter from Rudolf Alexander Schröder in which he declared himself to be Hesse's "traveling companion," and praised Hesse as the "heir of Germany's finest spirit."

Between the ages of fifty and sixty, Hesse published a large number of books in which he collected together the stories, essays, and other occasional writings, some of which had been published in collected editions before World War I, but many of which were still scattered among a large number of papers and journals. These books were the result of a critical second look at what he had written so far, and those he sifted out and preserved this time testify to the breadth of his interests and their underlying unity. *Picture Book,* published in 1926, consisted primarily of accounts of walking tours and journeys. Two years later came *Betrachtungen* (*Meditations*), dedicated to Hugo Ball, which in addition to many small pieces also contained his important wartime and post-war articles. In 1931, under the appropriate title *Weg nach Innen* (*Journey Inwards*), suggested by Ninon Hesse, *Siddhartha* and the three Klingsor stories were published in a joint edition; and a series of stories from three different books, *Diversions, Neighbors,* and *India,* were revised and collectively issued under the title *Kleine Welt* (*Small World*), dedicated to Hesse's three sons, Bruno, Heiner, and Martin. *Fabulierbuch* (*Fables*), a group of stories from the years 1904-1927, brought together a mixture of legends, fairy tales, and many delicately fashioned short stories which are entitled to a place in the great European tradition of story telling.

Gedenkblätter (*Memories*), a collection of memories, anecdotes, and homages first published in 1937, went into two further and enlarged editions. It consisted of a series of short pieces about people close to him, or whom he wished particularly to recall: his father, his brother Hans, and his sister Adele (always the closest to him), Franz Schall, Otmar Schoeck, Ernst Morgenthaler, Hugo Ball, unusual people he remembered from childhood, meetings with Christian Wagner, Raabe, and Schrempf. Hesse molded these very personal reminiscences into portraits that cleverly exhibited the central characteristics of each person, while never for a second losing sight of them as men and women of flesh and blood. It was his way of expressing the gratitude and love he felt towards them; this seems to have brought out the best in him as a writer, for these finely formed pieces stand comparison with the best of his writings.

There was another, and for Hesse more fundamental, motive behind this type of writing. He considered it a poet's duty to recall the past in this way. He once referred to the "Passionate struggle for recall," meaning that it was a function of the artist to defy the transience of things by "describing, pinning down, and handing on." Whatever escapes preservation in word or picture is a victim of decay. "The heart grieves over the transience of things but surrenders to it without resistance. But the spirit faces it fully armed and constantly renews its bid for victory."

"THE JOURNEY TO THE EAST" AND "THE GLASS BEAD GAME"

Hesse reached the high point of his creative endeavors with *The Glass Bead Game* (formerly known in English translation as *Magister Ludi*), a novel that drew upon a lifetime of work and experience, and that illuminated from a high vantage point all the milestones along the road that he had traveled so far. It is dedicated to "The Journeyers to the East," which we can interpret as Hesse's indication of the close relationship it has to *The Journey to the East,* a short novel he began in summer 1930 and completed in April 1931. In relation to *The Glass Bead Game* it is, as it were, an overture in which the basic theme is announced: the notion of service, the supra-personal hierarchy of a kingdom of the spirit, and, in the image of the League's

The epigraph of *The Glass Bead Game.*

archives, the synopsis of the cultural wealth of all peoples and countries subsequently projected in *The Glass Bead Game*. ". . . the paradox alone must always be accepted that the seemingly impossible must continually be attempted," wrote Hesse in *The Journey to the East*. It is a book in which the limits of time and space, the barriers that separate life and fiction, illusion and reality, are lifted. The action takes place in the inner world of spiritual experience. The League of Travelers, a strange brotherhood of exalted spirits from the past and men from the present, embark on a mysterious pilgrimage not to the geographical East but towards a goal that forms the travelers into a homogeneous spiritual community. "For our goal was not only the East, or rather the East was not only a country and something geographical, but it was the home and youth of the soul, it was everywhere and nowhere, it was the union of all times." The pilgrimage progresses through history and future, through time and space. "We moved towards the East, but we also traveled into the Middle Ages and the Golden Age; we roamed through Italy or Switzerland, but at times we also spent the night in the tenth century and dwelt with the patriarchs or the fairies . . . [we passed through] half of Europe and part of the Middle Ages."

The musician H. H. is also a member of the League, and his journey is presented as an allegorical representation of Hesse's own journey through life. It leads back into the past and the innocence of childhood and from there forward, illuminating the stages of his own growth to manhood, into error, doubt, and despair. Gradually the conviction that had held the League together begins to fade, he loses the track and, blaming others for his misfortune, wanders around in a foreign, lifeless reality. But he is driven onwards by compulsive longing, by "faith in the meaning and necessity of what he is doing." To his

136

amazement and satisfaction he discovers that, contrary to what he had thought, it was not the League that had foundered but he who had become a deserter from it by surrendering to weakness and doubt. The court of judgment at which he presents himself as accused and self-accused looks upon his error and fall only as a test and releases him. "Brother H. was led to despair in his test, and despair is the result of each earnest attempt to understand and vindicate human life. Despair is the result of each earnest attempt to go through life with virtue, justice, and understanding and to fulfill their requirements. Children live on one side of despair, the awakened on the other." Unlike Harry Haller, the Steppenwolf, H. survives the test of self-knowledge and so graduates to a new level of human existence.

The Journey to the East is full of symbol and allegory hiding a large number of references to events and people from the author's own life. But as Hesse confirmed in a letter to Alice Leuthold (whose house features in the book), the story can be fully appreciated without being aware of these allusions: "The reader does not need to be 'clear' about the symbolic content; he doesn't need to understand in the sense of 'clarify,' but should allow the images to sink into him and so more or less incidentally absorb that part of their meaning that has to do with images from real life. In this way the full effect unconsciously asserts itself . . . ."

The Journey to the East, dedicated to Hans C. Bodmer and his wife Elsy, was first published in 1931 in *Corona,* a journal edited by Martin Bodmer and Herbert Steiner. In the course of the next few years Hesse published excerpts from his new work, *The Glass Bead Game,* in both *Corona* and *Neue Rundschau.* From 1931 to 1942 work on this book was his primary concern. As early as 1935 he had described it in a letter as the ultimate goal of his life and work.

The photograph, taken by his son Martin, that Hesse called "The Rainmaker."

In the autumn of 1934 Hesse remarked in a letter: " 'The Rainmaker' [a section from *The Glass Bead Game*] was published in the spring in *Neue Rundschau* and in December another extract is to appear . . . of which so far only these two short sections are ready. This time work progresses very slowly—six- and twelve-month intervals between bouts. I have put in a lot of study as nourishment for my plan, which has absorbed and tormented me ever since I completed *The Journey to the East.* I have had to read a lot of eighteenth-century literature—in which connection I greatly enjoyed Oettinger, the Swabian pietist. And with the help of a nephew [Carlo Isenberg, Ferromonte in the book] I have studied classical music. Carlo is an organist and an expert on ancient music, as well as a collector of it. He stayed here with me for a few weeks and we hired a small piano . . ."

"Stunden im Garten" ("In the Garden"), a charming little idyll written in hexameters, provides us with an intimate picture of the slow emergence of *The Glass Bead Game.* First published in 1936 and designed and illustrated by Gunter Böhmer, a friend of Hesse and illustrator of many of his books, it describes the daily work in the garden. But Hesse was not only a gardener who watered his flowers and weeded their beds. His wife called him the charcoal burner, for his favorite pastime was making an earth fire, feeding it, dreaming and meditating in front of the smoldering embers. He saw fire as a sign of the return of all things to unity, of purification and refinement.

> Nowadays people are too busy to relax
> And to burn earth in the fire—who would pay them for it?
> But I am a poet and pay for it with considerable privation
> And even sacrifice; in return, God has permitted me
> Not just to live in these times but has also allowed time
> To cast me aside, leaving me in timeless space. Once that was
> Greatly prized; it was called withdrawal, or divine madness.
> But today it's considered worthless, because today time seems
> so valuable.
> To despise time is to blaspheme. The condition I refer to

Is called "introversion" by the specialists
And is used to describe the behavior of a weakling
Who runs away from life's responsibilities
And loses himself in the private pleasures of his dreams,
And whom no mature person can take seriously.

When the fire is burned out, its ashes are mixed with
earth and then shaken through a sieve:

. . . and quite unconsciously my shaking
Of the sieve slipped into a particular rhythm
Which in turn provoked the welcome memory of
A piece of music which I hummed to myself without
At first identifying its name, or that of its composer.
Then suddenly it came to me: Mozart, an oboe quartet . . .
And this gave rise to a game which I have been playing for
    years
Called the glass bead game, an enchanting invention
Whose framework is music and whose basis is meditation.
Joseph Knecht is the master to whom I am indebted for
My knowledge of this pleasing pastime. In times of joy
It is my play and my pleasure; in times of suffering and
    trouble,
It is my comfort, and means of reflection, and here by the
    fire,
Shaking my sieve, I play it often, my glass bead game,
But not nearly as well as Knecht.

. . .

While in front of the stable here the huge sunflowers look at
    me
And behind the vine-clad boughs the distance breathes the
    midday blue,
I hear music and see past and future mankind,
See custom and poet and seeker and artist in one accord

Building a hundred-doored cathedral of the spirit—once
  later
I will set it down, the day has not yet come.

The Glass Bead Game was completed on April 29, 1942. The manuscript remained in Berlin for seven months, but in spite of the efforts made on its behalf by Peter Suhrkamp, publisher and friend, the book could not be printed in Germany. It was therefore published in Switzerland. Only a few copies crossed the border, and those that did became treasured possessions to be passed from hand to hand.

In a letter to Rudolf Pannwitz written in 1955, Hesse recalled some memories from the time of its gestation: "The idea that originally fired me was the notion of reincarnation as the vehicle through which to express stability in change, the continuity in tradition, and the life of the spirit generally. And then one day, many years before I actually started writing, I visualized a particular but supratemporal life history: I imagined a man who in several incarnations experiences the great epochs of human history." Between that first plan and actually starting to write lay "years of moderate peace following a serious crisis, and for Germany and Europe also, exhausted by the war, it was a time of recuperation in which to recover some joy in life . . . but then . . . from the speeches of Hitler and his ministers, and from their newspapers and pamphlets, there arose a sort of poisonous gas, a wave of meanness, deceit, and uninhibited status-seeking, an air that was intolerable to breathe. It didn't require the appalling horrors that followed several years later to place me once again, as previously during the war years, on the edge of the abyss; this poisoned atmosphere, this debasement of language, this dethronement of truth, was quite

Making a bonfire.

enough. Once again, the air was poisoned and life was in the balance. The time had come for me to summon up all my powers of survival and to test and strengthen such faith as I had . . . In the midst of these threats and dangers surrounding my physical and spiritual existence I grasped for the remedy all artists use, namely work, and so returned afresh to the old plan, which, however, changed considerably under the pressures of the moment. Two things mattered to me: first, to construct an area, a refuge, a fortress, in which I could breathe and live in defiance of the poison around me; secondly, to express the spirit's resistance against the barbaric powers and, if possible, to encourage my friends across the border in their resistance and perseverance.

"But to construct this area in which I could find refuge, strength, and courage, it was not enough to evoke and lovingly portray just any period from the past—which is what my earlier plan would have entailed. I saw that in defiance of the leering present I had to demonstrate that the kingdom of the spirit and of the soul existed and was invincible. Realizing this, my plan changed direction towards a utopian presentation, an image projected into the future, the evil present charmed into a past that had survived the rigors of its own day. To my astonishment, the Province of Castalia emerged of itself. It didn't need to be thought up or constructed. Without my knowing it, it had taken shape within me long ago. I had already found the sanctuary I had been looking for."

Hesse's primary objective was to contrast an anarchic world with a place (called Castalia in the book) in which measure, spiritual order, discipline, and reverence reigned. He wanted to put forward models; and just as for centuries Plato's Academy had served as a worthwhile ideal, so Castalia was to become a model for a world that had lost its integrity. Though the Province of Castalia is visualized in terms of the future, it is not to be understood as a future era, nor as prophecy or utopian postulate, but as a timeless concept that possesses its own inner reality and whose purpose is to present the possibility of a life of the spirit.

143

The Glass Bead Game is subtitled "A tentative sketch of the life of Magister Ludi Joseph Knecht together with Knecht's posthumous writings." It takes place several centuries on from our own and is a description of life in Castalia, a place reminiscent of Goethe's "Pädagogische Provinz" (from the *Wanderjahre*). The nineteenth and twentieth centuries, described as the "feuilletonistic age," and their undisiciplined individualism, wars, and moral degradation, have been overcome. Reacting to the despair they felt on account of the decline of civilization, a group of people came together with the purpose of remaining true to the higher values and recreating a world in which these would be properly respected. The result was the establishment of an "Order" whose members lived like monks, rejected the pursuit of worldly success and all creative artistic activity, devoting themselves primarily to the study of music, mathematics, and philology, with the ultimate purpose of achieving a synthesis of all disciplines and cultures. At the center of their activity is the glass bead game, played through the medium of a highly developed and secret language, according to its own rules and grammar, and symbolic of the unity of the spirit, of the homogeneity of all concepts and of all values created by art and civilization.

"The Glass Bead Game is thus a mode of playing with the total contents of our culture; it plays with them as, say, in the great age of the arts a painter might have played with the colors on his palette. All the insights, noble thoughts, and works of art that the human race has produced in its creative eras, all that subsequent periods of scholarly study have reduced to concepts and converted into intellectual property—on all this immense body of intellectual values the Glass Bead Game player plays like the organist on an organ. And this organ has attained an almost unimaginable perfection; its manuals and pedals range over the entire

144

intellectual cosmos; its stops are almost beyond number. Theoretically this instrument is capable of producing in the Game the entire intellectual content of the universe.''

Years of practice are needed to play the game properly, only a few perfect the art, and only one can be *Magister Ludi,* a position that empowers him to devise and direct the great public games, the Order's quasi-liturgical ceremonial performances.

The Order of Castalians is isolated within the State and has its own hierarchy. But the State recognizes it and guarantees its material security. In return, the Order offers places in its elite schools for the country's most gifted sons.

This is the context in which Joseph Knecht plays out his life, his story being told retrospectively on the basis of old documents and records. Musically very gifted, at the age of twelve the young Knecht is admitted to one of Castalia's elite schools, having first passed a special test. He completes his education at the school as one of its best students and, after a few years of further study on his own, enters the Order. Quickly becoming a member of its inner elite, he is sent for a period of two years to the seminary of Mariafels in order to cement his connection to the Benedictines. In Mariafels he meets Father Jacobus, a noted historian, and through him is introduced to the nature of the historical world. Returning to his own Order, he is elected Magister Ludi and so achieves the highest rank in the intellectual hierarchy. He proves himself to be an excellent teacher and an outstanding player of the glass bead game. But now the Order's enthusiastic protagonist begins to realize that even Castalia does not signify absolute value: it is just another example of the historical mode of existence and as such is also a victim of transience. It becomes increasingly clear to him that change and progress are necessary to preservation and persever-

145

F

ance, that all achievement "is condemned to wither away if it loses the ability to increase and transform itself." With this knowledge, and convinced that he has now exhausted whatever the Order had to offer him, he decides to leave. In spite of the Order's objections, he resigns his office, goes out into the world, and becomes tutor to the son of a school friend. But shortly after starting in his new post he meets his death by drowning in a mountain lake.

Even a much more detailed description of the story could do only poor justice to its real content and to the particular atmosphere its author creates. Hesse unfolds his story like a complicated fugue, an interplay of the forces of nature and the forces of the mind. But intensely complicated though it is, a few of its basic themes must be mentioned here.

The Glass Bead Game begins with "A General Introduction to its History for the Layman," an introductory chapter that precedes the story of Knecht's life. This chapter is headed by an epigraph that Hesse first drafted as early as 1933 and which was subsequently rendered into Latin by Franz Schall (Clangor), one of his closest friends, and then edited by Feinhals (Collofino), another friend. In English it reads: ". . . For although in a certain sense and for light-minded persons non-existent things can be more easily and irresponsibly represented in words than existing things, for the serious and conscientious historian it is just the reverse. Nothing is harder, yet nothing is more necessary, than to speak of certain things whose existence is neither demonstrable nor probable. The very fact that serious and conscientious men treat them as existing things brings them a step closer to existence and to the possibility of being born."

Hesse confirmed in a letter to Emil Staiger that this statement holds a key to an understanding of the book:

146

"The evocation of an idea, the presentation of a realization of it, is in effect one step nearer its actual realization (*paululum appropinquant*)." The idea evoked and presented as reality is the Province of Castalia with its Order of glass bead game players. Hesse has the Order emerge in history at the end of "the warlike age," and ascribes to it the function of preserving the works of the spirit for the country and the world. In order to uphold "order, norm, reason, law, and measure," the players have foresworn politics, economics, and other worldly occupations, including family life. By giving the world "teachers, books, and methods," by fulfilling the function of "gauger of intellectual and spiritual weights and measures," and by making themselves responsible for the proper mainten-

With Theodor Heuss.

147

ance of the intellectual functions, they render a considerable and necessary service to the State that makes their existence possible.

But this function can only be performed by an elite. Only the best men are selected, as only they will have the intellectual and spiritual powers to suppress their individuality so that they may then align themselves absolutely with the Order's hierarchy, and devote their lives exclusively to "the spirit and the truth."

Among the primary means by which members of the Order achieve this attitude is the practice of meditation, through which the individual can, as it were, neutralize himself and so permit his soul to become immersed in itself, thus becoming conscious of its participation in the unity of life. The practice of "meditative wisdom and harmony" and that of "objectivity and love of truth" constitute the two basic principles on which the spirit of the Province of Castalia is founded.

The final and most complex expression of this spirit is the glass bead game, which is the concrete expression "of the concept of the inner unity of all man's intellectual efforts, of the concept of universality." The game itself is never precisely described. Therein lies its mystery and symbolic content.

> To keep, in metaphor, in symbol and psalm,
> Reminders of that former sacred reverence,

is, to use the language of one of Knecht's posthumous poems, the function of the Order, and in his great debate with Plinio Designori he explains that the glass bead game unites the three principles of "science, homage to beauty, and meditation."

The highest and finest disposition to be gained from playing the glass bead game is serenity. For this reason "a proper Glass Bead Game player ought to be drenched in cheerfulness as a ripe fruit is drenched in its sweet juices. He ought above all to possess the cheerful serenity of music, for, after all, music is nothing but an act of courage, a serene, smiling, striding forward and dancing through the terrors and flames of the world, and festive offering of a sacrifice . . . Such cheerfulness is neither frivolity nor complacency; it is supreme insight and love, affirmation of all reality, alertness on the brinks of all depths and abysses; it is a virtue of saints and of knights; it is indestructible and only increases with age and nearness to death. It is the secret of beauty and the real substance of all art. The poet who praises the splendors and terrors of life in the dance-measures of his verse; the musician who sounds them in a pure, eternal present—these are bringers of light, the increasers of joy and brightness on earth, even if they lead us first through tears and stress. Perhaps the poet whose verses gladdened us was a sad solitary, and the musician a melancholic dreamer; but even so their work shares in the cheerful serenity of the gods and the stars. What they give us is no longer their darkness, their suffering or fears, but a drop of pure light, eternal cheerfulness. Even though whole people and languages have attempted to fathom the depths of the universe in myths, cosmogonies, and religions, their supreme, their ultimate attainment has been this cheerfulness.''

The words "serene" and "serenity" remind us of Schiller, a writer with whom Hesse otherwise had very little intellectual kinship. During the last years of his life these two words occurred frequently in letters and conversations, being used to signify a relaxed and exalted state of mind. Hesse saw the possession of serenity as a sign of real freedom.

"Man is truly himself only when at play."

Hesse saw serenity as an indication of the classical

temperament, as something that reached its zenith in the music that stretches from Purcell to Schubert. Serenity was to be acquired through familiarity with such music. "Classical music as gesture signifies knowledge of the tragedy of the human condition, affirmation of human destiny, courage, cheerful serenity." The notion of music as transforming power is one that runs through the whole book.

"Perfect music has its cause. It arises from equilibrium. Equilibrium arises from righteousness, and righteousness arises from the meaning of the cosmos. Therefore one can speak about music only with a man who has perceived the meaning of the cosmos. Music is founded on the harmony between heaven and earth, on the concord of obscurity and brightness."

At the end of his discussion with Designori, Knecht begins to play the piano: ". . . carefully, very softly, played a movement from the Purcell sonata which was one of Father Jacobus's favorite pieces. The notes fell into the stillness like drops of golden light, so softly that along with them the song of the old fountain in the yard could be heard. Gently, austerely, sparingly, sweetly, the lovely separate voices met and mingled; bravely and gaily they paced their tender rondo through the void of time and transitoriness, for a little while making the room and the night hour vast as the universe. And when the friends bade each other good night, the guest's face had changed and brightened, although his eyes had filled with tears."

Knecht's path led him beyond Castalia. To keep faith with his own convictions he had to desert the Order which formerly in fierce discussions with Plinio he had defended to the hilt, and whose existence he had tried to substantiate and vindicate in his discussions with Father Jacobus. But none of this affects the Province of Castalia, which is still intact at the end of the book, though by then it is clear that it, too, has its limitations—that it, too, is subject to the relativity of the historical world. For Tegularius, who, as the most extreme exponent of Castalia's refined spirituality, becomes Knecht's opponent despite his dependence on him, the study of history is quite simply unworthy of the attention of a genuine Castalian. But through Father Jacobus, through whom Hesse expresses his homage to the great historian Jacob Burckhardt, Knecht experienced "history not as an academic discipline but as reality, as life" and as "analogous to the transformation and development of a man's own life into history." "Hungry for reality, for tasks and deeds," he leaves the Order, not to become a world reformer "but a teacher and educator, in the first instance as an educator with only one pupil . . . He places all his energy and all his gifts at the service of one person." True to his name (Knecht means servant), he becomes a servant and thereby becomes totally free.

In the course of the decisive discussion in which Knecht explains his decision to Master Alexander, the Order's President, he says: "My life, I resolved, ought to be a perpetual transcending, a progression from stage to stage; I wanted it to pass through one area after the next, leaving each behind, as music moves on from theme to theme, from tempo to tempo, playing each out to the end, completing each and leaving it behind, never tiring, never sleeping, forever wakeful, forever in the present."

"Each of us is merely one human being, merely an experiment, a way station. But each of us should be on the way towards perfection, should be striving to reach the center, not the periphery," said the Music Master to Knecht, his young pupil. These comments are reminiscent of thoughts from the Demian period, but also from the Siddhartha period, particularly when he continues: "There is truth, my boy. But the doctrine you desire, absolute, perfect dogma that alone provides wisdom, does

151

not exist. Nor should you long for a perfect doctrine, my friend. Rather, you should long for the perfection of yourself. The deity is within *you*, not in ideas and books. Truth is lived, not taught.''

In *Demian* we read: "Only the ideas that we really *live* have any value.'' Spirit and life in constant alternation and tension form one of the most important themes in Hesse's thought and work. He sees man as something superior to institution, dogma, and doctrine. Man must follow his own law, must act according to the free exercise of responsibility and be prepared always for new experiences and ventures.

Hesse expressed this fundamental notion in "Stufen'' ("Stages''), a poem that was originally called "Transzendieren'' ("To Transcend''), and that was written on a May night in 1941 when, following a lengthy illness, he was able for the first time in many weeks to think of work.

As every flower fades and as all youth
Departs, so life at every stage,
So every virtue, so our grasp of truth,
Blooms in its day and may not last forever.
Since life may summon us at every age
Be ready, heart, for parting, new endeavor,
Be ready bravely and without remorse
To find new light that old ties cannot give.
In all beginnings dwells a magic force
For guarding us and helping us to live.

Serenely let us move to distant places
And let no sentiments of home detain us.
The Cosmic Spirit seeks not to restrain us
But lifts us stage by stage to wider spaces.
If we accept a home of our own making,
Familiar habit makes for indolence.

We must prepare for parting and leave-taking
Or else remain the slaves of permanence.

Even the hour of our death may send
Us speeding on to fresh and newer spaces,
And life may summon us to newer races.
So be it, heart: bid farewell without end.

The Glass Bead Game was published in Germany in 1946, three years after its publication in Switzerland, and had a particularly powerful and enduring effect. Whereas his earlier books were more like prognoses and diagnoses of the times, the book was therapeutic in construction, despite its criticism of contemporary civilization. He wanted to point to the healing powers that can lead from chaos to order. The book's content, though not so much its form, aroused widespread and excited debate, and there were numerous attempts to interpret this very complex piece of writing.

Hesse was frequently urged to prepare a collected edition of his poems. But he resisted the idea for a long time: "for, given the enormous number of them—many of them very similar to one another—I just could not believe there would be a demand for a perpetuation of them all. If anything were to be done to them, then it should surely be selecting, sifting, and pruning.

"However, I did appreciate that the purpose of a collected edition was quite different from that of a selection, and that for me, too, a collected edition could serve some useful purpose: as a statement of what I have lived and done, as a final surrender of all the material without retouching or suppressing any of it, as affirmation of the whole, including all its failings and questionable aspects—

153

Viele Länder und Städte weiß ich noch warten,
Aber niemals wohl wird der Wälder Nacht,
Wird der wilde gährende Urweltgarten
Wieder mich lockern und schrecken mit seiner Pracht.

Hier in dieser unendlichen leuchtenden Wildnis
War ich weiter als je entrückt von der Menschenwelt —
O und niemals sah ich so nah und unverstellt
Meiner eigenen Seele gespiegeltes Bildnis.

DER BLÜTENZWEIG

Immer hin und wider
Strebt der Blütenzweig im Winde,
Immer auf und nieder
Strebt mein Herz gleich einem Kinde
Zwischen hellen, dunkeln Tagen,
Zwischen Wollen und Entsagen.

Bis die Blüten sind verweht
Und der Zweig in Früchten steht,
Bis das Herz, der Kindheit satt,
Seine Ruhe hat
Und bekennt: voll Lust und nicht vergebens
War das unruhvolle Spiel des Lebens.

REISELIED

Sonne leuchte mir ins Herz hinein,
Wind verweh mir Sorgen und Beschwerden!
Tiefere Wonne weiß ich nicht auf Erden,
Als im Weiten unterwegs zu sein.

221

A corrected proof from *Gedichte.*

and these would turn out to be more than just a matter of
unhappy rhymes and metrical faults.''

Nevertheless, it remained a project that he was unwill-
ing to undertake, though he finally did so in deference to

persistent demand. *Die Gedichte* (*Poems*), as the complete edition was called, was published in 1942 by Fretz and Wasmuth, the Zurich publishers who, in agreement with Peter Suhrkamp, issued those books by Hesse that Suhrkamp was unable to publish in Germany.

With the exception of about 150 poems written either in fun or for particular occasions, and a few poems from *Crisis* that were purely private in character, *Poems* includes every poem Hesse wrote: about 600 altogether, written over a period of nearly fifty years and previously available only in a dozen different books.

Because the poems appear in chronological order it is easy to follow the poet's overall development from the *Romantic Songs* of the nineteen-year-old to the work of the sixty-year-old. Inasmuch as every poem Hesse wrote amounted to a highly personal statement about himself, the collected poems together constitute the story of his inner life.

As a lyricist, Hesse wrote in the tradition of German poetry that was rooted in the folk song and that progressed via Goethe to the Romantics and Mörike. Hesse saw himself as a link in a chain and had neither the inner urge nor the ambition to start a fresh movement: "With a few exceptions, I was satisfied with the traditional form, the proven style, and never felt any desire to start something new, to be *avant garde,* a pioneer . . ."

Hesse's early poems, poems of longing, aimless wandering, solitude, and homesickness, make use of the traditional moods and imagery typical of the Romantics. "Home" and "dream" are words that constantly recur as Hesse looks back over his shoulder at the lost joys of youth and the security he then enjoyed. Hesse was nothing if not sentimental, and his sensitive nature suffered much from the experience of reality and the conflict between nature and spirit. Despairingly, he sought redemption and a way out of an apparently meaningless world.

His experience of psychoanalysis and his encounter with the wisdom of the East enabled him to find his way to the interior (*Journey Inwards*), to the heart of the world (*Herz der Welt*), through which he came to appreciate the indestructibility of the inner self.

He found refuge in the maternal principle as the expression of permanence and eternal rebirth. The eternal mother was a symbol that fascinated him and that came to the fore in many of his poems. But he also found that it is a symbol that needs its opposite, the paternal principle, representing "the spirit" against the maternal principle's representation of nature. "Reflections," a poem that expresses an idea central to all Hesse's thought, begins with the line "Divine and eternal is the spirit," and continues:

> *But nature does not satisfy—*
> *The paternal spark of the immortal spirit*
> *Breaks through its mother-magic*
> *And leads the child to manhood,*
> *Extinguishes innocence and arouses us to arms and con-*
> *   science.*
> *Thus between mother and father*
> *Thus between body and spirit*
> *Dallies creation's most fragile child,*
> *The trembling soul of man, capable of suffering*
> *As no other being, and capable of the very highest:*
> *Of believing, loving hope.*

Hesse is driven by the desire for permanence, by the "thirst for being.—To stiffen into stone! To persevere! That is what we always and actively long for," he wrote in "Klage" ("Lamentation"), another poem. But as nothing on this earth is eternal except "change" and "flight," safe ground is only discovered when permanence is recognized precisely in the continuity of change. Awareness of this lends his later work, poems such as "Organ Music" or "Zu einer Toccata von Bach" ("A Toccata by Bach"), the equilibrium and composure so lacking in his early poems. To invest the fleeting image with immortality, to give it spirit and permanence, Hesse saw as the poet's function and particular talent.

Chinese

Moonlight that through opalescent cloudbreaks
Can hardly make out the bamboo shapes
Paints smoothly and cleanly in the water
The reflection of the high humped-back bridge.

These are images that we dearly love,
On the lightless ground of world and night
Magically swimming, magically depicted,
With us now, and then extinguished.

Under the mulberry tree the drunken poet
Who wields a brush as ably as a tankard
Portrays the moon night that enthuses him
Through gentle lights and drifting shadows.

His rapid brush strokes delineate
The moon and clouds and all those images
That flash across the beholder's mind.
By praising the fleeting images
And by experiencing them
The tender poet gives them
Spirit and permanence.

They will remain immortal.

157

THE FINAL YEARS

Writing in March 1933 to Rudolf Jakob Humm, Hesse said: ". . . if I am now more consciously than ever a solitary and a 'dreamer,' then at least I *am* conscious of it and see it not as a curse but as a role to fulfill. I do, of course, have my own type of community and conviviality. Each year I receive a few thousand letters, all from young people (most of them under twenty-five), and many of them come to visit me. Almost without exception they are talented if complex young people, with a larger than average awareness of themselves as individuals, and as such are bewildered by the conventional requirements of so-called civilization. Some are pathological, others so magnificent that privately I have made them bearers of what hope I still have in the continuation of the German spirit. Having neither the authority nor the right, I can act neither as pastor nor as doctor to this minority of lively but somewhat imperiled young souls. But insofar as my empathy suffices, I encourage in each of them that which separates them from the conventional norms, and try to show them the meaning of maintaining this sort of distance." In a letter written at the same time, Hesse wrote: "For twenty years these letters have been the only real proof of the meaning of my existence and work, though they have also been my daily burden and trial."

The flood of letters increased sharply in the years immediately following World War II. People of all ages and classes turned to him for advice, information, and help, expressing their most private concerns and needs, problems that frequently had no connection at all with his writing, but which they nevertheless confidently presented to him much as though he were their doctor or private confessor.

About 1955.

Hesse was the recipient of "a ceaseless stream of all types of misery—from gentle complaint and timid request to angry and sullen assertions of cynical despair."

Conscious of their historical value, Hesse bequeathed

some of these letters to a library, and in 1951 he published a selection from his own replies.

This collection of letters is quite different from the published letters of contemporary writers and exhibits the effect a writer had on a small but very significant section of his public in a way that is without parallel in modern times. Several twentieth-century writers have been great letter-writers, but whereas the usual emphasis of, say, Thomas Mann or Hugo von Hofmannsthal was on an exchange of correspondence in which a dialogue was carried on by two like-minded people, this is not the case with Hesse; almost exclusively, his letters—at least those of them so far published—are once and for all replies, and his letters to friends and relatives with whom he had lasting connections are more in the nature of straightforwardly informative communications. That Hesse, like no other writer of his

times, was inundated by a flood of extremely personal letters, most of them demonstrating a considerable degree of confidence in him, may well be taken as proof that the intimately confessional aspect of his writing appealed strongly to a great many readers, because Hesse was expressing things in them that sorely needed clarification. "When I first read a book of yours I found many things that I had sensed myself more or less consciously," a German student wrote to him; and a gymnast in Tokyo informed Hesse that ". . . the more I read them [Hesse's books], the more I find myself in them. And now I am convinced that the person who understands me best is in Switzerland and that I am never out of his sight . . ."

Hesse wrote thousands of letters in response to this flood, until his correspondence occupied "the greater part of his working day." He wasn't always happy about it, and the labor often left him weary and ill-humored, but he never gave up. He rarely failed to answer a letter, and even on the day after his eighty-fifth birthday he was up by 7:30 a.m. to start on his replies to the morning's postbag of 900 congratulatory letters.

"Your letter finds me suffering from eye-trouble and buried beneath a heavy mail and so I shall be brief. But an answer seems required as I understand your appeal and feel moved by it." Time and again, Hesse had to refuse the role of *Führer* his correspondents would have thrust upon him, just as he always declined to offer pat answers or provide life-recipes in response to the problems presented to him. "I can no more answer your questions than I can my own. I am as much oppressed by life's brutality as you are. But I have faith that life's meaninglessness can be overcome insofar as I am always able to assert a meaning for my own life. I believe I am not responsible for the meaningfulness or meaninglessness of life, but that I *am* responsible for what I do with the life I've got."

Not all his answers were pleasant ones. Sometimes, and

161

particularly in the case of importunate writers, he could be very terse, but he was always honest, and always took his correspondents seriously, never fobbing them off with platitudes or rhetoric.

Hesse's letters were written for their recipients, not for publication. They are not examples of fine writing but they constituted, particularly in the second half of his life, a considerable part of his total output and express his innermost feelings, his attitude towards life, and his wish to be an influence for good.

"Renewed greetings from an old individualist," he wrote to Gide in January 1951. He remained a loner to the end. "I could never have enough privacy." His natural reserve was an aspect of his awareness that writing required peace, patience, and constant preparedness, a process of concentration that could not do without the protection of domestic security. His handwritten manuscripts, particularly those of his longer works, carry amazingly few corrections, thus showing how intense and concentrated his work was: he would not start to write until what he wanted to set down on paper was clear in his mind. As a rule, he would first write everything out in longhand and then type it when he had finished. Any necessary corrections or changes were made at this stage. One sees that the urge for seclusion that removed him from public life was not "a spiritual or intellectual need, but a physical one, a husbanding of resources." He lived apart, but through conscience and easily excited sensibility he participated in world events and suffered under the world's crises more intensely than many of those directly concerned.

The end of the war and the restoration of postal services brought Hesse a huge mailbag. In the space of a few months he received "well over a thousand letters, many of them containing appalling reports of events in Germany during the preceding years . . . and each of them was a claim not only on over-strained eyes and weary head, but also poured into me a ceaseless and heartbreaking flood of laments, questions, requests, accusations, and appeals for help." As far as he was able, he tried to offer practical assistance. But he was also irritated and disappointed to see that so few Germans were aware of what had really happened. "The German people as a whole feels in no way responsible for what it has done to the world and to itself."

Hesse held back from public protest and collective action, but felt obliged to make his own position unequivocally clear in his personal style: "Instead of worrying about what blame might attach to you and about how you might better yourself, you are content nobly to pronounce judgment on others," he wrote tersely in one of his letters. "This is not the way forward. You also maintain that you lost the war because you were not so well armed as your enemies. That is just one of those still-thriving German lies. You lost the war, that satanically and insanely pursued act of aggression towards your neighbors, not for that reason . . . but because once again the world found the German urge to conquer and kill intolerable. And if you have the whole world against you, you naturally lose. And having lost, instead of trying to learn from your mistakes, you gripe about how others behaved . . . This is my first and last letter to you. You'll learn nothing from it because you don't want to, but unfortunately I was obliged to write it."

When in 1946 Hesse's *Brief nach Deutschland* (*Letter to Germany*), a piece of very sharp criticism of the attitudes typical of many Germans, was published against his will in the *Neue Zeitung,* he received a large number of abusive and unpleasant letters. In his response to these, *Antwort auf Schmähbriefe aus Deutschland* (*A Reply to Defamatory Letters from Germany*), in the *Zürcher Zeitung,* he wrote:

"Ever since 1914, when Germany launched an unjust war to the accompaniment of an increasingly uninhibited propaganda, I have from time to time, starting in autumn 1914 and most recently in spring 1946, penned an appeal or a warning to those in Germany capable of listening, and in return have been laughed at, vilified, and abused. Your letter, by no means one of the worst, is but one of several thousand abusive letters I have had from Germany over a period of thirty-two years . . . Many people maintain that one should not expect a nation that is suffering grievously to learn anything. For myself, I could not imagine a time in which self-awareness and self-analysis are more necessary than when affliction and humiliation are at their worst."

In the same year, Hesse was awarded the Nobel Prize for Literature. Bad health prevented him from making the journey to Sweden to accept the prize in person, but in his speech of thanks he said: "I feel united to you all, but primarily through the fundamental notion that inspired the Nobel Foundation, the idea of the supranationality and internationality of the spirit and its duty to serve not war and destruction but peace and reconciliation. The prize you have awarded me is also a recognition of the German language and of Germany's contribution to civilization, and this I see as a gesture of reconciliation and good will . . ."

Other honors followed. He was awarded the City of Frankfurt's Goethe Prize in 1946, was elected an honorary doctor of the University of Berne in 1947, and in 1950 the City of Brunswick accorded him the Wilhelm Raabe Prize. In 1955 he was elected to the Peace Class of the Order *Pour la merite,* and in the autumn of the same year he received the Peace Prize of the German Book Trade.

His books were translated into numerous languages. In Japan, where his books were particularly popular, two editions of his collected works were issued in addition to sixty-five editions of individual books.

During his last years, Hesse left Montagnola only for very short intervals. Only his summer holidays in Oberengadin interrupted the rhythm of his secluded year. But this is not to say that his house became an ivory tower, let alone a bucolic idyll, nor even the final resting place of a spent force. Numerous contacts kept him in close touch with the outside world, and with the easing of travel restrictions after the war, he had so many visitors that he was left with almost no time at all in which to get on with his own work. Indeed, it became so bad that he had to keep people away, and to this end nailed to the door of his house this excerpt from the writings of Meng Hsia:

When a man has grown old and has fought his fight, it is proper that he should be left in peace to familiarize himself with death. He has no need of people. He knows them already and has seen enough of them.

What he needs is peace.
It is not seemly to seek out such a man, to speak to him, to plague him with chatter.
The proper course is to pass by the gate of his house as though no one lived there.

In this way Hesse protected himself from the importunate and the curious, while at the same time making it possible to offer hospitality to guests of his own choice. For the house was seldom empty of visitors. He invited his Swabian relatives to visit him, particularly his two sisters, Adele and Marulla; relatives of his wife also came, now fugitives from Rumania. Friends and visitors from all over the world were received. "Though 1947 brought little to

165

rejoice about," he wrote in December that year, "there were one or two delightful occasions, particularly the pleasure of seeing Thomas Mann again, and a little later Martin Buber and Hans Carossa."

Ernst Morgenthaler stayed with Hesse for a few weeks in order to paint his portrait. Both writer and painter spoke enthusiastically of the sittings that followed. And one day, out of the blue, André Gide arrived. During the two-hour conversation he hardly once took his eyes off a basket in a corner of the room where a cat lay with her two-week-old kittens. "His was the calm and controlled gaze of a man well accustomed to society; and in his gaze, and in the persistence with which he constantly sought out his object, one could detect the great power that governed his life and that drove him to Africa, England, Germany, and Greece. This gaze, this great openness and familiarity with the miracles of the world, was capable of love and sympathy without falling into sentimentality. No matter how fully he threw himself into something, he always knew what he was doing. His primary motivation was his thirst for knowledge."

Gide's son-in-law, Jean Lambert, translated *The Journey to the East* into French, and Gide himself contributed an essay on Hesse by way of a Foreword. "It is a joy and a comfort to have in you a lover and defender of freedom, personality, the personal viewpoint, and individual responsibility," Hesse wrote in his last letter to Gide.

Hesse was particularly pleased to see his cousin Wilhelm Gundert again for the first time in twenty-four years. Several of the friends he had made as a young man also came to see him, including his close friend Otto Hartmann. Hartmann died only a few weeks after the visit, which Hesse described as a "day of autumn serenity, full of close memories; a day of love and tenderness leavened by humor."

One of his most welcome visitors was the publisher Peter Suhrkamp, who had suffered so dreadfully in prison and in a concentration camp, and who was now in the process of setting up his own publishing house, having for so long and in such trying circumstances carried on old Samuel Fischer's business. Hesse became one of Suhrkamp's authors. This led to the publication on his seventy-fifth birthday (1952) of a very fine edition of his collected writings (*Gesammelte Dichtungen*) in six volumes, to which a seventh volume was added in 1957. In an obituary notice for Suhrkamp, who died on March 31, 1959, Hesse wrote: "his whole life revolved about two poles: on the one hand, ceaseless and enterprising activity undertaken out of a desire to create something worthwhile, and on the other a longing to escape the world and live in peace and seclusion . . . whenever in conversation or reading I come across references to the 'true' or 'genuine' Germany, Peter's tall, gaunt figure comes immediately to mind."

After the Second World War, Hesse spent the hottest summer weeks of every year in Sils Maria in Engadin, whose countryside he became very fond of. "I have seen many country areas and have admired most of them, but of the very few that have impressed me profoundly and that with growing familiarity blossomed gradually into second homes, none has ever appealed to me more strongly than that of Upper Engadin."

The Glass Bead Game is Hesse's most important work and it was also his last major book. *Traumfährte* (*Dream Journeys*), dedicated to "The painter Ernst Morgenthaler in gratitude for many rewarding hours spent in his company in summer 1945," is a collection of fairy tales, allegories, and parodies, written between 1910 and 1932, and published in 1945. It includes the autobiographical sketches "The Magician's Childhood" and "Curriculum Vitae," the delightful "Schwäbische Parodie" ("Swabian Parody"), and an enchanting fairy tale "Vogel" ("Bird"). These prose pieces, twelve in all, are autobiographical testimonies that combine charmingly presented personal detail with profundity and irony.

Hesse's writing after the war consisted of short stories, essays, a handful of poems, diary entries, meditations, open letters, published privately and in newspapers, and eventually collected in two separate volumes, *Späte Prosa* (*Late Prose*) and *Beschwörungen* (*Evocations*), the latter dedicated to his wife, Ninon. These fine prose pieces are a mixture of straight description, evocations of times past, and original thought. A masterpiece of its type is *Die Beschreibung einer Landschaft* (*The Description of a Region*), in which with conscious feelings of inadequacy Hesse attempted to describe with maximum accuracy the park land and countryside around Marin which he visited in the winter of 1946-47 for a health cure.

Although Hesse's life was a series of crises and new beginnings, his work and thought show an amazing degree of consistent development. From *Hermann Lauscher* on through all his subsequent books he tenaciously pursued his basic theme. In one way or another, all his chief characters represent their creator: "I see Knulp, Demian, Siddhartha, Klingsor, Steppenwolf, and Goldmund as brothers of one another, each a variation of my central theme," he informed one of his readers in 1930. Twenty-four years later he described this theme as the defense of the personality: "From Camenzind to Steppenwolf and Josef Knecht, they can all be interpreted as a defense (sometimes also as an SOS) of the personality, of the individual self." But this was not only his chosen theme as a writer: it was also the fundamental principle of his life and thought. He stood guarantor for the indestructibility of the personal, intellectual, and spiritual life. That is the secret of his widespread impact. His significance is not to be determined by subjecting his output to literary-critical analysis, for it extends far beyond the literary sphere. Hesse was acutely aware of the apparent meaninglessness of his own life and the crises of the Western world, and suffered considerably from both. He felt as though he stood at the edge of the abyss and that the depths were threatening to claim him for good, and his evocation in his later work of a world of order, measure, reverence, and harmony, was his way of making a bid for mastery of the powers of threatening chaos.

He saw language as the strongest tool in such a bid. His style was always clear, simple, and disciplined. Those who do not know how difficult it is to achieve such simplicity of style sometimes find Hesse disappointing to read. Concerning this, Gide wrote in his Foreword to the French edition of *The Journey to the East:* "In Hesse's writing it is not the interplay of the emotions, or the thought, that is toned down, but solely the mode of expression. His language is simple and its measured style is a reflection of his feeling for decency, reserve, harmony, and—in relation to the cosmos—for the interdependence of things; his writing exhibits a restrained irony such as, so it seems to me, very few German writers are capable of, and whose total absence so often spoils the books of many authors who take themselves so terribly seriously."

On Christmas night of the year 1961 Hesse wrote a poem called "Einst vor Tausend Jahren" ("Once, a Thousand Years Ago"), whose first verse runs as follows:

> *Restless, and anxious for another journey*
> *Awakened from a broken dream*
> *I hear in the night*
> *The familiar rustlings of my bamboos.*

Hesse yearned to be on his way again, but this time into the infinite.

> *I would like to spread my wings*
> *And escape the bondage that encircles me.*

He showed the poem to his wife, who was horrified to see such obvious signs of his longing for death.

Hesse was ill throughout the winter of 1961, though he

On his eighty-fifth birthday.

felt secure enough in the hands of Dr. Molo, whose
patient he had been for the past eleven years. Hesse was
unaware that for some time he had been suffering from
leukemia.

On his eighty-fifth birthday, Montagnola elected him an
honorary citizen. He was delighted to accept, and in his
speech of thanks reminded his hosts of how he had so
often sung the praises of Ticino and the Collina d'Oro
during the forty years and more that he had lived among
them. The birthday itself was celebrated with his family
and a few friends in Faido am Gotthard. Max Wassmer, a
faithful friend of many years, was the host.

Though the illness that had plagued him throughout the
winter appeared to have abated, his doctor advised him
not to make his customary annual trip to Sils Maria. "One

171

more summer and another winter" are the final words of "Das Knarren eines geknickten Astes" ("The Creaking of a Crooked Branch") his last poem. That was in the first days of August. On the evening of August 8, he listened to a Mozart sonata, and his wife read aloud to him as she had been doing every evening. The next morning Hesse died in his sleep of a cerebral hemorrhage.

He was buried in the cemetery of S. Abbondio in the afternoon of August 11. The funeral oration was delivered by Dekan Volter, a friend with whom he had attended the Maulbronn seminary seventy years earlier. Two of his sons and two grandsons carried the coffin from the chapel to the cemetery.

A few weeks later Rudolf Alexander Schröder and Louis Moilliet also died; and Ernst Morgenthaler followed them in the autumn.

One of Hesse's last poems, "written on an April night" in the spring of 1961, ends with these lines:

What you loved and what you strove for
What you dreamed and what you lived through,
Do you know if it was joy or suffering?
G sharp and A flat, E flat or D sharp—
Are they distinguishable to the ear?

CHRONOLOGY

1877   Born July 2 in Calw, Württemberg, second
           child of Johannes and Marie (née Gundert)
           Hesse.

1881–1886 Basle, where Johannes Hesse was teaching.

1886   The family returns to Calw.

1890–1891 Attends the preparatory school in Göppingen.

1891   Passes the Swabian *Landexamen* in July.

1891–1892 Attends the Maulbronn Seminary.

1892   Runs away from Maulbronn in March. From
           May onwards attends various schools (Bad
           Boll, Stetten im Remstal, Basle).

1892–1893 Attends the Gymnasium in Bad Cannstatt.

1893–1894 Gives up a bookshop apprenticeship and as-
           sists his father.

1894–1895 Apprentice mechanic in Heinrich Perrot's
           clock workshops, Calw.

1895–1898 Apprentice in a Tübingen bookshop.

1898–1899 Promoted to assistant.

1899   *Romantische Lieder. Eine Stunde hinter Mit-
           ternacht.*

1899–1903 Works in a Basle bookshop. Travels in Swit-
           zerland.

1901   First Italian journey (Florence, Ravenna,
           Venice). *Hinterlassene Schriften und Gedichte von
           Hermann Lauscher.*

1902   Death of his mother. *Gedichte.*

1903   Second Italian journey.

1904   *Peter Camenzind,* Hesse's first literary success.

Marries Maria Bernoulli. Is awarded the Bauernfeld Prize.

1904–1912 Lives in Gaienhofen on the Bodensee. Writes and contributes to numerous journals (*Simplicissimus, Rheinlande, Neue Rundschau,* and others). Visits Italy. Lecture tours.

1905 Birth of first child, Bruno.

1906 *Unterm Rad.*

1907 Builds his own house in Gaienhofen. *Diesseits.*

1907–1912 Co-edits *März.*

1908 *Nachbarn.*

1909 Birth of second child, Heiner.

1910 *Gertrud.*

1911 *Unterwegs.* Birth of third child, Martin. Visits India.

1912 *Umwege.*

1912–1919 Berne.

1913 *Aus Indien.*

1914 *Rosshalde.*

1914–1919 Works for the Prisoners of War Welfare Organization, Berne. Edits two journals for German prisoners and publishes a series of books for them.

1915 *Knulp. Am Weg. Musik des Einsamen.*

1916 Death of his father. Wife and son Martin seriously ill. Psychoanalysis in Lucerne. *Schön ist die Jugend.*

1919 *Demian,* first published under the pseudonym Emil Sinclair. Returns the Fontane Prize awarded to "Sinclair." *Kleiner Garten. Märchen. Zarathustras Wiederkehr.*

1919–1922 Co-edits *Vivos Voco.*

1919 Leaves Berne to live on his own in Montagnola.

1920 *Gedichte des Malers. Klingsors Letzter Sommer. Wanderung.*

1921	*Ausgewählte Gedichte.*
1922	*Siddhartha.*
1923	*Sinclairs Notizbuch.* Adopts Swiss citizenship.
1924	Marries Ruth Wenger, January.
1925	*Kurgast.*
1925–1931	Spends every winter in Zurich.
1926	*Bilderbuch.* Is elected a member of the Prussian Academy of Writers.
1927	*Die Nürnberger Reise. Der Steppenwolf.* Publication of Hugo Ball's biography of Hesse.
1928	*Betrachtungen. Krisis.*
1929	*Trost der Nacht. Eine Bibliothek der Weltliteratur.*
1930	*Narziss und Goldmund.* Resigns from the Prussian Academy of Writers.
1931	Marries Ninon Dolbin in November. Moves into a new house in Montagnola built for him as life tenant by Hans C. Bodmer. Begins work on *Glasperlenspiel.*
1932	*Die Morgenlandfahrt.*
1936	*Stunden im Garten.* Is awarded the Gottfried Keller Prize.
1937	*Gedenkblätter. Neue Gedichte.*
1942	*Die Gedichte.*
1943	*Glasperlenspiel.*
1945	*Traumfährte.*
1946	Receives the Frankfurt Goethe Prize. *Dank an Goethe. Krieg und Frieden.* Awarded Nobel Prize.
1947	Becomes honorary doctor of the University of Berne.
1950	Receives Wilhelm Raabe Prize.
1951	*Späte Prosa. Briefe.*
1952	*Gesammelte Dichtungen* (6 vols.).
1955	Receives the Peace Prize of the German Book Trade. *Beschwörungen. Gesammelte Schriften* (7 vols.).
1962	Dies in Montagnola on August 9.

BIBLIOGRAPHY

Demian. Translated from the German by W. J. Strachan. London: Peter Owen, 1958 (5th imp. 1970); Panther Books, 1969.

Gertrude. Translated from the German by Hilda Rosner. London: Peter Owen, 1955 (5th imp. 1972).

The Glass Bead Game. Translated from the German, *Das Glasperlenspiel,* by Richard and Clara Winston. London: Jonathan Cape, 1970. (Previously translated as *Magister Ludi.*)

If the War Goes On. Translated from the German, *Krieg und Frieden* (in preparation). London: Jonathan Cape, 1972 (provisional).

The Journey to the East. Translated from the German, *Die Morgenlandfahrt,* by Hilda Rosner. London: Peter Owen, 1956 (4th imp. 1972).

Klingsor's Last Summer. Translated from the German, *Klingsors Letzter Sommer* (and including *A Child's Heart* and *Klein and Wagner*), by Richard and Clara Winston. London: Jonathan Cape, 1971.

Knulp. English translation in preparation. London: Jonathan Cape, 1972 (provisional).

Narziss and Goldmund. Translated from the German by Geoffrey Dunlop. London: Peter Owen, 1959 (5th imp. 1970); Harmondsworth, Middx: Penguin Books, 1971. (Previously translated as *Death and the Lover* and *Goldmund.*)

Peter Camenzind. Translated from the German by W. J. Strachan. London: Peter Owen, 1961 (3rd imp. 1970).

Poems. Selected and translated from the German by James Wright. London: Jonathan Cape, 1971.

The Prodigy. Translated from the German, *Unterm Rad,* by W. J. Strachan. London: Peter Owen, 1952 (4th imp. 1970). (Also published in U.S. as *Beneath the Wheel.*)

Rosshalde. Translated from the German by Ralph Manheim. London: Jonathan Cape, 1971.

Siddhartha. Translated from the German by Hilda Rosner. London: Peter Owen, 1954 (7th imp. 1971).

Steppenwolf. Translated from the German by Basil Creighton, revised by Walter Sorell. Harmondsworth, Middx: Penguin Books, 1965. (Originally published London: Martin Secker, 1929.)